PUZZLE PACK
for
Out of the Dust

based on the book by
Karen Hesse

Written by
William T. Collins

© 2005 Teacher's Pet Publications
All Rights Reserved

The materials in this packet are copyrighted
by Teacher's Pet Publications, Inc.

These pages may be duplicated by the purchaser
for use in the purchaser's own classroom.

Copying any of these materials and distributing them
for any other purpose is a violation of the copyright laws.

© 2005 Teacher's Pet Publications, Inc.
www.tpet.com

INTRODUCTION
If you already own the LitPlan for this title, this Puzzle Pack will refresh your Unit Resource Materials and Vocabulary Resource Materials sections plus give you additional materials you can substitute into the tests. If you do not already have a complete LitPlan, these pages will give you some supplemental materials to use with your own plan. There are two main groups of materials: one set for unit words (such as characters' names, symbols, places, etc.) and one set for vocabulary words associated with the book.

WORD LIST
There is a word list for both the unit words and the vocabulary words. These lists show you which words are being used in the materials and the clues or definitions being used for those words. You may want to give students a word list with clues/definitions to help them, or you may want students to only have a word list (without clues/definitions) if you want them to work a little harder. Both are available for duplication. The word lists can also be your "calling key" for the bingo games.

FILL IN THE BLANK AND MATCHING
There are 4 each of the fill in the blank and matching worksheets for both the unit and vocabulary words. These pages can be used either as extra worksheets for students or as objective parts of a unit test. They can be done individually if students need extra help or as a whole class activity to review the material covered.

MAGIC SQUARES
The magic squares not only reinforce the material covered but also work on reasoning and math skills. Many teachers have told us that their students really enjoy doing these!

WORD SEARCH PUZZLES
The word search words go in all directions, as indicated on your answer keys. Two of the word search puzzles have the clues listed rather than the words. This makes the puzzle a little more difficult, but it reinforces the material better. Two word search puzzles have words only for students who find the clue puzzles too difficult.

CROSSWORD PUZZLES
Both unit and vocabulary word sections have 4 crossword puzzles.

BINGO CARDS
There are 32 individual bingo cards for the unit words and 32 individual bingo cards for the vocabulary words. You can use your word list as a "call list," calling the words at random and marking them off of your list as you go, or you could use the flash cards by cutting them apart and drawing the words at random from a hat (or box or whatever). To make a better review, you might ask for the definition and spelling of each word as you call it out—or you could call out the definitions and have students tell you the words they need to look for on the puzzle.

JUGGLE LETTERS
The vocabulary juggle letter game is intended to help students learn the spellings of the words. One sheet has the definitions listed on it as an extra help for students who need it or to reinforce the definitions if you choose to do so.

FLASH CARDS
We've included a set of vocabulary flash cards you can duplicate, cut, and fold for your students. Some teachers make a few sets for general use by the class; others make a set for each student. Some teachers duplicate them for each student and have the students cut & fold their own. You can cut out just the words and put them in a hat, have each student pick out one word and write the definition and a sentence for that word. Students then swap words and papers, with the next student adding a sentence of his own under the last one. You can have students swap as many times as you like. Each time the student will read the sentences written prior to his own and then add a sentence. You can cut out the words and definitions separately and play "I Have; Who Has?" Each student in the room draws a word and definition. The first student says, "I have (the name of the word). Who has the definition?" The student with the definition reads it then says, "I have (the name of the vocabulary word she has). Who has the definition?" The round continues until all words and definitions have been given.

Out Of The Dust Word List

No.	Word	Clue/Definition
1.	ARLEY	The music promoter: ___ Wanderdale
2.	BAYARD	Billie Jo's father's last name
3.	BUTTERFLY	The opera Billie Jo didn't know was Madame ___
4.	CEREUS	Kind of plant that bloomed at midnight and died at dawn
5.	CRADDOCK	Mad Dog's last name
6.	CRANBERRY	Billie Jo didn't know how to make ___ sauce.
7.	DIONNE	Last name of the Canadian quintuplets
8.	ELLIE	Billie Jo's Aunt ___
9.	ELZIRE	First name of the quintuplets' mother
10.	FLOR	Joe De La ___ was Billie Jo's neighbor.
11.	FRANKLIN	Billie Jo's brother who died young
12.	FREELAND	Miss ___ was Billie Jo's teacher.
13.	GUYMON	Produce deliverer: Pete ___
14.	HARDLY	Mr. ___ was the local grocer.
15.	JIM	The man cleaning up the Crystal Hotel was ___ Martin.
16.	KELBY	Billie Jo's last name
17.	LIVIE	The Killian daughter Billie Jo was friends with.
18.	LOUISE	Woman Billie Jo's father got engaged to
19.	LUCAS	The funeral of Grandma ___ was important to the Kelbys.
20.	NOBLE	Mr. ___ quarreled with Mr. Romney.
21.	NYE	Last name of Haydon who was an old-time Oklahoman
22.	POLLY	Billie Jo's mother: ___ Kelby
23.	POND	Billie Jo's mother wanted her husband to dig a ___.
24.	POPPIES	What was growing on the graves of soldiers in France
25.	POWER	Billie Jo's father got a job with Wireless ___.
26.	REUBEN	___ Killian left home to make his own way
27.	RICE	Last name of the local doctor
28.	ROMNEY	Mr. ___ quarreled about killing rabbits.
29.	RUSSIAN	Type of thistle Joe De La Flor would feed cattle
30.	VERA	Arley's wife
31.	WHEAT	The crop Billie Jo's father tried to grow

Out Of The Dust Fill In The Blanks 1

_____   1. First name of the quintuplets' mother

_____   2. Mr. ___ quarreled about killing rabbits.

_____   3. The opera Billie Jo didn't know was Madame ___

_____   4. Kind of plant that bloomed at midnight and died at dawn

_____   5. Billie Jo's mother wanted her husband to dig a ___.

_____   6. Mr. ___ was the local grocer.

_____   7. The Killian daughter Billie Jo was friends with.

_____   8. The funeral of Grandma ___ was important to the Kelbys.

_____   9. The music promoter: ___ Wanderdale

_____   10. Type of thistle Joe De La Flor would feed cattle

_____   11. Billie Jo's father's last name

_____   12. Mad Dog's last name

_____   13. The crop Billie Jo's father tried to grow

_____   14. Miss ___ was Billie Jo's teacher.

_____   15. The man cleaning up the Crystal Hotel was ___ Martin.

_____   16. Arley's wife

_____   17. Billie Jo didn't know how to make ___ sauce.

_____   18. Joe De La ___ was Billie Jo's neighbor.

_____   19. Last name of the Canadian quintuplets

_____   20. ___ Killian left home to make his own way

Out Of The Dust Fill In The Blanks 1 Answer Key

ELZIRE	1. First name of the quintuplets' mother
ROMNEY	2. Mr. ___ quarreled about killing rabbits.
BUTTERFLY	3. The opera Billie Jo didn't know was Madame ___
CEREUS	4. Kind of plant that bloomed at midnight and died at dawn
POND	5. Billie Jo's mother wanted her husband to dig a ___.
HARDLY	6. Mr. ___ was the local grocer.
LIVIE	7. The Killian daughter Billie Jo was friends with.
LUCAS	8. The funeral of Grandma ___ was important to the Kelbys.
ARLEY	9. The music promoter: ___ Wanderdale
RUSSIAN	10. Type of thistle Joe De La Flor would feed cattle
BAYARD	11. Billie Jo's father's last name
CRADDOCK	12. Mad Dog's last name
WHEAT	13. The crop Billie Jo's father tried to grow
FREELAND	14. Miss ___ was Billie Jo's teacher.
JIM	15. The man cleaning up the Crystal Hotel was ___ Martin.
VERA	16. Arley's wife
CRANBERRY	17. Billie Jo didn't know how to make ___ sauce.
FLOR	18. Joe De La ___ was Billie Jo's neighbor.
DIONNE	19. Last name of the Canadian quintuplets
REUBEN	20. ___ Killian left home to make his own way

Out Of The Dust Fill In The Blanks 2

_____ 1. Joe De La ___ was Billie Jo's neighbor.

_____ 2. The crop Billie Jo's father tried to grow

_____ 3. Billie Jo's mother wanted her husband to dig a ___.

_____ 4. Billie Jo's father got a job with Wireless ___.

_____ 5. Last name of Haydon who was an old-time Oklahoman

_____ 6. Billie Jo didn't know how to make ___ sauce.

_____ 7. The Killian daughter Billie Jo was friends with.

_____ 8. Kind of plant that bloomed at midnight and died at dawn

_____ 9. Mr. ___ quarreled with Mr. Romney.

_____ 10. Mr. ___ quarreled about killing rabbits.

_____ 11. Billie Jo's last name

_____ 12. Mad Dog's last name

_____ 13. Billie Jo's Aunt ___

_____ 14. Last name of the local doctor

_____ 15. The funeral of Grandma ___ was important to the Kelbys.

_____ 16. Billie Jo's father's last name

_____ 17. Mr. ___ was the local grocer.

_____ 18. The music promoter: ___ Wanderdale

_____ 19. The opera Billie Jo didn't know was Madame ___

_____ 20. Arley's wife

Out Of The Dust Fill In The Blanks 2 Answer Key

FLOR	1. Joe De La ___ was Billie Jo's neighbor.
WHEAT	2. The crop Billie Jo's father tried to grow
POND	3. Billie Jo's mother wanted her husband to dig a ___.
POWER	4. Billie Jo's father got a job with Wireless ___.
NYE	5. Last name of Haydon who was an old-time Oklahoman
CRANBERRY	6. Billie Jo didn't know how to make ___ sauce.
LIVIE	7. The Killian daughter Billie Jo was friends with.
CEREUS	8. Kind of plant that bloomed at midnight and died at dawn
NOBLE	9. Mr. ___ quarreled with Mr. Romney.
ROMNEY	10. Mr. ___ quarreled about killing rabbits.
KELBY	11. Billie Jo's last name
CRADDOCK	12. Mad Dog's last name
ELLIE	13. Billie Jo's Aunt ___
RICE	14. Last name of the local doctor
LUCAS	15. The funeral of Grandma ___ was important to the Kelbys.
BAYARD	16. Billie Jo's father's last name
HARDLY	17. Mr. ___ was the local grocer.
ARLEY	18. The music promoter: ___ Wanderdale
BUTTERFLY	19. The opera Billie Jo didn't know was Madame ___
VERA	20. Arley's wife

Out Of The Dust Fill In The Blanks 3

_____ 1. Woman Billie Jo's father got engaged to

_____ 2. The music promoter: ___ Wanderdale

_____ 3. Miss ___ was Billie Jo's teacher.

_____ 4. Arley's wife

_____ 5. The opera Billie Jo didn't know was Madame ___

_____ 6. First name of the quintuplets' mother

_____ 7. What was growing on the graves of soldiers in France

_____ 8. The funeral of Grandma ___ was important to the Kelbys.

_____ 9. Last name of Haydon who was an old-time Oklahoman

_____ 10. ___ Killian left home to make his own way

_____ 11. The man cleaning up the Crystal Hotel was ___ Martin.

_____ 12. Billie Jo's Aunt ___

_____ 13. Last name of the Canadian quintuplets

_____ 14. Kind of plant that bloomed at midnight and died at dawn

_____ 15. Billie Jo's mother: ___ Kelby

_____ 16. Billie Jo's last name

_____ 17. Mad Dog's last name

_____ 18. Billie Jo's mother wanted her husband to dig a ___.

_____ 19. Produce deliverer: Pete ___

_____ 20. Mr. ___ quarreled about killing rabbits.

Out Of The Dust Fill In The Blanks 3 Answer Key

LOUISE	1. Woman Billie Jo's father got engaged to
ARLEY	2. The music promoter: ___ Wanderdale
FREELAND	3. Miss ___ was Billie Jo's teacher.
VERA	4. Arley's wife
BUTTERFLY	5. The opera Billie Jo didn't know was Madame ___
ELZIRE	6. First name of the quintuplets' mother
POPPIES	7. What was growing on the graves of soldiers in France
LUCAS	8. The funeral of Grandma ___ was important to the Kelbys.
NYE	9. Last name of Haydon who was an old-time Oklahoman
REUBEN	10. ___ Killian left home to make his own way
JIM	11. The man cleaning up the Crystal Hotel was ___ Martin.
ELLIE	12. Billie Jo's Aunt ___
DIONNE	13. Last name of the Canadian quintuplets
CEREUS	14. Kind of plant that bloomed at midnight and died at dawn
POLLY	15. Billie Jo's mother: ___ Kelby
KELBY	16. Billie Jo's last name
CRADDOCK	17. Mad Dog's last name
POND	18. Billie Jo's mother wanted her husband to dig a ___.
GUYMON	19. Produce deliverer: Pete ___
ROMNEY	20. Mr. ___ quarreled about killing rabbits.

Out Of The Dust Fill In The Blanks 4

_____ 1. Mr. ___ was the local grocer.

_____ 2. Mr. ___ quarreled with Mr. Romney.

_____ 3. Woman Billie Jo's father got engaged to

_____ 4. Mr. ___ quarreled about killing rabbits.

_____ 5. The opera Billie Jo didn't know was Madame ___

_____ 6. Mad Dog's last name

_____ 7. The funeral of Grandma ___ was important to the Kelbys.

_____ 8. Joe De La ___ was Billie Jo's neighbor.

_____ 9. Last name of Haydon who was an old-time Oklahoman

_____ 10. The crop Billie Jo's father tried to grow

_____ 11. Billie Jo's mother wanted her husband to dig a ___.

_____ 12. Billie Jo's brother who died young

_____ 13. The music promoter: ___ Wanderdale

_____ 14. What was growing on the graves of soldiers in France

_____ 15. Last name of the Canadian quintuplets

_____ 16. Billie Jo's father got a job with Wireless ___.

_____ 17. Billie Jo didn't know how to make ___ sauce.

_____ 18. The Killian daughter Billie Jo was friends with.

_____ 19. Kind of plant that bloomed at midnight and died at dawn

_____ 20. ___ Killian left home to make his own way

Out Of The Dust Fill In The Blanks 4 Answer Key

HARDLY	1. Mr. ___ was the local grocer.
NOBLE	2. Mr. ___ quarreled with Mr. Romney.
LOUISE	3. Woman Billie Jo's father got engaged to
ROMNEY	4. Mr. ___ quarreled about killing rabbits.
BUTTERFLY	5. The opera Billie Jo didn't know was Madame ___
CRADDOCK	6. Mad Dog's last name
LUCAS	7. The funeral of Grandma ___ was important to the Kelbys.
FLOR	8. Joe De La ___ was Billie Jo's neighbor.
NYE	9. Last name of Haydon who was an old-time Oklahoman
WHEAT	10. The crop Billie Jo's father tried to grow
POND	11. Billie Jo's mother wanted her husband to dig a ___.
FRANKLIN	12. Billie Jo's brother who died young
ARLEY	13. The music promoter: ___ Wanderdale
POPPIES	14. What was growing on the graves of soldiers in France
DIONNE	15. Last name of the Canadian quintuplets
POWER	16. Billie Jo's father got a job with Wireless ___.
CRANBERRY	17. Billie Jo didn't know how to make ___ sauce.
LIVIE	18. The Killian daughter Billie Jo was friends with.
CEREUS	19. Kind of plant that bloomed at midnight and died at dawn
REUBEN	20. ___ Killian left home to make his own way

Out Of The Dust Matching 1

___ 1. CEREUS   A. Last name of the local doctor
___ 2. FRANKLIN   B. The funeral of Grandma ___ was important to the Kelbys.
___ 3. POLLY   C. Last name of Haydon who was an old-time Oklahoman
___ 4. ELLIE   D. Produce deliverer: Pete ___
___ 5. NYE   E. Kind of plant that bloomed at midnight and died at dawn
___ 6. ARLEY   F. The music promoter: ___ Wanderdale
___ 7. BAYARD   G. Billie Jo's father's last name
___ 8. KELBY   H. Type of thistle Joe De La Flor would feed cattle
___ 9. GUYMON   I. The crop Billie Jo's father tried to grow
___ 10. LUCAS   J. The man cleaning up the Crystal Hotel was ___ Martin.
___ 11. FREELAND   K. ___ Killian left home to make his own way
___ 12. RUSSIAN   L. Billie Jo's brother who died young
___ 13. ELZIRE   M. Billie Jo's Aunt ___
___ 14. LOUISE   N. The opera Billie Jo didn't know was Madame ___
___ 15. POPPIES   O. Billie Jo's mother wanted her husband to dig a ___.
___ 16. FLOR   P. Woman Billie Jo's father got engaged to
___ 17. RICE   Q. Joe De La ___ was Billie Jo's neighbor.
___ 18. POND   R. What was growing on the graves of soldiers in France
___ 19. ROMNEY   S. Mr. ___ quarreled about killing rabbits.
___ 20. BUTTERFLY   T. Billie Jo's mother: ___ Kelby
___ 21. NOBLE   U. Miss ___ was Billie Jo's teacher
___ 22. WHEAT   V. Billie Jo's father got a job with Wireless ___.
___ 23. POWER   W. Mr. ___ quarreled with Mr. Romney.
___ 24. JIM   X. First name of the quintuplets' mother
___ 25. REUBEN   Y. Billie Jo's last name

Out Of The Dust Matching 1 Answer Key

E - 1. CEREUS	A.	Last name of the local doctor
L - 2. FRANKLIN	B.	The funeral of Grandma ___ was important to the Kelbys.
T - 3. POLLY	C.	Last name of Haydon who was an old-time Oklahoman
M - 4. ELLIE	D.	Produce deliverer: Pete ___
C - 5. NYE	E.	Kind of plant that bloomed at midnight and died at dawn
F - 6. ARLEY	F.	The music promoter: ___ Wanderdale
G - 7. BAYARD	G.	Billie Jo's father's last name
Y - 8. KELBY	H.	Type of thistle Joe De La Flor would feed cattle
D - 9. GUYMON	I.	The crop Billie Jo's father tried to grow
B - 10. LUCAS	J.	The man cleaning up the Crystal Hotel was ___ Martin.
U - 11. FREELAND	K.	___ Killian left home to make his own way
H - 12. RUSSIAN	L.	Billie Jo's brother who died young
X - 13. ELZIRE	M.	Billie Jo's Aunt ___
P - 14. LOUISE	N.	The opera Billie Jo didn't know was Madame ___
R - 15. POPPIES	O.	Billie Jo's mother wanted her husband to dig a ___.
Q - 16. FLOR	P.	Woman Billie Jo's father got engaged to
A - 17. RICE	Q.	Joe De La ___ was Billie Jo's neighbor.
O - 18. POND	R.	What was growing on the graves of soldiers in France
S - 19. ROMNEY	S.	Mr. ___ quarreled about killing rabbits.
N - 20. BUTTERFLY	T.	Billie Jo's mother: ___ Kelby
W - 21. NOBLE	U.	Miss ___ was Billie Jo's teacher.
I - 22. WHEAT	V.	Billie Jo's father got a job with Wireless ___.
V - 23. POWER	W.	Mr. ___ quarreled with Mr. Romney.
J - 24. JIM	X.	First name of the quintuplets' mother
K - 25. REUBEN	Y.	Billie Jo's last name

Out Of The Dust Matching 2

___ 1. ELLIE   A. Miss ___ was Billie Jo's teacher.
___ 2. FLOR   B. Mad Dog's last name
___ 3. ROMNEY   C. Arley's wife
___ 4. CRADDOCK   D. Billie Jo's last name
___ 5. REUBEN   E. What was growing on the graves of soldiers in France
___ 6. ARLEY   F. Produce deliverer: Pete ___
___ 7. WHEAT   G. The man cleaning up the Crystal Hotel was ___ Martin.
___ 8. RUSSIAN   H. Billie Jo's mother wanted her husband to dig a ___.
___ 9. RICE   I. ___ Killian left home to make his own way
___ 10. DIONNE   J. Billie Jo didn't know how to make ___ sauce.
___ 11. LIVIE   K. Joe De La ___ was Billie Jo's neighbor.
___ 12. JIM   L. Type of thistle Joe De La Flor would feed cattle
___ 13. CRANBERRY   M. Mr. ___ quarreled about killing rabbits.
___ 14. NOBLE   N. Billie Jo's Aunt ___
___ 15. BAYARD   O. Last name of the local doctor
___ 16. POND   P. Billie Jo's father's last name
___ 17. VERA   Q. Kind of plant that bloomed at midnight and died at dawn
___ 18. FREELAND   R. Billie Jo's mother: ___ Kelby
___ 19. KELBY   S. Mr. ___ was the local grocer.
___ 20. CEREUS   T. The Killian daughter Billie Jo was friends with.
___ 21. GUYMON   U. The crop Billie Jo's father tried to grow
___ 22. POPPIES   V. Last name of the Canadian quintuplets
___ 23. POLLY   W. Mr. ___ quarreled with Mr. Romney.
___ 24. FRANKLIN   X. The music promoter: ___ Wanderdale
___ 25. HARDLY   Y. Billie Jo's brother who died young

Out Of The Dust Matching 2 Answer Key

N - 1.	ELLIE	A.	Miss ___ was Billie Jo's teacher.
K - 2.	FLOR	B.	Mad Dog's last name
M - 3.	ROMNEY	C.	Arley's wife
B - 4.	CRADDOCK	D.	Billie Jo's last name
I - 5.	REUBEN	E.	What was growing on the graves of soldiers in France
X - 6.	ARLEY	F.	Produce deliverer: Pete ___
U - 7.	WHEAT	G.	The man cleaning up the Crystal Hotel was ___ Martin.
L - 8.	RUSSIAN	H.	Billie Jo's mother wanted her husband to dig a ___.
O - 9.	RICE	I.	___ Killian left home to make his own way
V - 10.	DIONNE	J.	Billie Jo didn't know how to make ___ sauce.
T - 11.	LIVIE	K.	Joe De La ___ was Billie Jo's neighbor.
G - 12.	JIM	L.	Type of thistle Joe De La Flor would feed cattle
J - 13.	CRANBERRY	M.	Mr. ___ quarreled about killing rabbits.
W - 14.	NOBLE	N.	Billie Jo's Aunt ___
P - 15.	BAYARD	O.	Last name of the local doctor
H - 16.	POND	P.	Billie Jo's father's last name
C - 17.	VERA	Q.	Kind of plant that bloomed at midnight and died at dawn
A - 18.	FREELAND	R.	Billie Jo's mother: ___ Kelby
D - 19.	KELBY	S.	Mr. ___ was the local grocer.
Q - 20.	CEREUS	T.	The Killian daughter Billie Jo was friends with.
F - 21.	GUYMON	U.	The crop Billie Jo's father tried to grow
E - 22.	POPPIES	V.	Last name of the Canadian quintuplets
R - 23.	POLLY	W.	Mr. ___ quarreled with Mr. Romney.
Y - 24.	FRANKLIN	X.	The music promoter: ___ Wanderdale
S - 25.	HARDLY	Y.	Billie Jo's brother who died young

Out Of The Dust Matching 3

___ 1. FLOR   A. Mr. ___ quarreled with Mr. Romney.
___ 2. ELZIRE   B. Last name of the local doctor
___ 3. JIM   C. Billie Jo's Aunt ___
___ 4. LIVIE   D. Miss ___ was Billie Jo's teacher.
___ 5. VERA   E. Produce deliverer: Pete ___
___ 6. CRADDOCK   F. Billie Jo's brother who died young
___ 7. WHEAT   G. Last name of the Canadian quintuplets
___ 8. BUTTERFLY   H. Mad Dog's last name
___ 9. BAYARD   I. The music promoter: ___ Wanderdale
___10. ELLIE   J. Type of thistle Joe De La Flor would feed cattle
___11. POWER   K. Joe De La ___ was Billie Jo's neighbor.
___12. NOBLE   L. Last name of Haydon who was an old-time Oklahoman
___13. DIONNE   M. The opera Billie Jo didn't know was Madame ___
___14. ARLEY   N. The crop Billie Jo's father tried to grow
___15. CRANBERRY   O. Arley's wife
___16. REUBEN   P. ___ Killian left home to make his own way
___17. GUYMON   Q. The funeral of Grandma ___ was important to the Kelbys.
___18. POLLY   R. Billie Jo's mother: ___ Kelby
___19. LUCAS   S. Billie Jo's father got a job with Wireless ___.
___20. RUSSIAN   T. The man cleaning up the Crystal Hotel was ___ Martin.
___21. FREELAND   U. Billie Jo's father's last name
___22. RICE   V. The Killian daughter Billie Jo was friends with.
___23. POND   W. Billie Jo didn't know how to make ___ sauce.
___24. FRANKLIN   X. First name of the quintuplets' mother
___25. NYE   Y. Billie Jo's mother wanted her husband to dig a ___.

Out Of The Dust Matching 3 Answer Key

K - 1.	FLOR	A.	Mr. ___ quarreled with Mr. Romney.
X - 2.	ELZIRE	B.	Last name of the local doctor
T - 3.	JIM	C.	Billie Jo's Aunt ___
V - 4.	LIVIE	D.	Miss ___ was Billie Jo's teacher.
O - 5.	VERA	E.	Produce deliverer: Pete ___
H - 6.	CRADDOCK	F.	Billie Jo's brother who died young
N - 7.	WHEAT	G.	Last name of the Canadian quintuplets
M - 8.	BUTTERFLY	H.	Mad Dog's last name
U - 9.	BAYARD	I.	The music promoter: ___ Wanderdale
C - 10.	ELLIE	J.	Type of thistle Joe De La Flor would feed cattle
S - 11.	POWER	K.	Joe De La ___ was Billie Jo's neighbor.
A - 12.	NOBLE	L.	Last name of Haydon who was an old-time Oklahoman
G - 13.	DIONNE	M.	The opera Billie Jo didn't know was Madame ___
I - 14.	ARLEY	N.	The crop Billie Jo's father tried to grow
W - 15.	CRANBERRY	O.	Arley's wife
P - 16.	REUBEN	P.	___ Killian left home to make his own way
E - 17.	GUYMON	Q.	The funeral of Grandma ___ was important to the Kelbys.
R - 18.	POLLY	R.	Billie Jo's mother: ___ Kelby
Q - 19.	LUCAS	S.	Billie Jo's father got a job with Wireless ___.
J - 20.	RUSSIAN	T.	The man cleaning up the Crystal Hotel was ___ Martin.
D - 21.	FREELAND	U.	Billie Jo's father's last name
B - 22.	RICE	V.	The Killian daughter Billie Jo was friends with.
Y - 23.	POND	W.	Billie Jo didn't know how to make ___ sauce.
F - 24.	FRANKLIN	X.	First name of the quintuplets' mother
L - 25.	NYE	Y.	Billie Jo's mother wanted her husband to dig a ___.

Out Of The Dust Matching 4

___ 1. VERA   A. The man cleaning up the Crystal Hotel was ___ Martin.
___ 2. DIONNE   B. Billie Jo's mother wanted her husband to dig a ___.
___ 3. ELLIE   C. The opera Billie Jo didn't know was Madame ___
___ 4. LUCAS   D. Billie Jo's brother who died young
___ 5. GUYMON   E. Mr. ___ quarreled about killing rabbits.
___ 6. ROMNEY   F. Last name of the Canadian quintuplets
___ 7. FREELAND   G. Woman Billie Jo's father got engaged to
___ 8. CEREUS   H. Mr. ___ was the local grocer.
___ 9. HARDLY   I. Billie Jo's Aunt ___
___ 10. ARLEY   J. Produce deliverer: Pete ___
___ 11. CRANBERRY   K. First name of the quintuplets' mother
___ 12. WHEAT   L. Billie Jo's father's last name
___ 13. KELBY   M. The Killian daughter Billie Jo was friends with.
___ 14. REUBEN   N. Last name of the local doctor
___ 15. NYE   O. ___ Killian left home to make his own way
___ 16. POLLY   P. Billie Jo's last name
___ 17. BAYARD   Q. The crop Billie Jo's father tried to grow
___ 18. JIM   R. Miss ___ was Billie Jo's teacher.
___ 19. BUTTERFLY   S. Billie Jo didn't know how to make ___ sauce.
___ 20. RICE   T. The funeral of Grandma ___ was important to the Kelbys.
___ 21. POND   U. The music promoter: ___ Wanderdale
___ 22. ELZIRE   V. Kind of plant that bloomed at midnight and died at dawn
___ 23. FRANKLIN   W. Billie Jo's mother: ___ Kelby
___ 24. LIVIE   X. Last name of Haydon who was an old-time Oklahoman
___ 25. LOUISE   Y. Arley's wife

Out Of The Dust Matching 4 Answer Key

Y - 1.	VERA	A.	The man cleaning up the Crystal Hotel was ___ Martin.
F - 2.	DIONNE	B.	Billie Jo's mother wanted her husband to dig a ___.
I - 3.	ELLIE	C.	The opera Billie Jo didn't know was Madame ___
T - 4.	LUCAS	D.	Billie Jo's brother who died young
J - 5.	GUYMON	E.	Mr. ___ quarreled about killing rabbits.
E - 6.	ROMNEY	F.	Last name of the Canadian quintuplets
R - 7.	FREELAND	G.	Woman Billie Jo's father got engaged to
V - 8.	CEREUS	H.	Mr. ___ was the local grocer.
H - 9.	HARDLY	I.	Billie Jo's Aunt ___
U -10.	ARLEY	J.	Produce deliverer: Pete ___
S -11.	CRANBERRY	K.	First name of the quintuplets' mother
Q -12.	WHEAT	L.	Billie Jo's father's last name
P -13.	KELBY	M.	The Killian daughter Billie Jo was friends with.
O -14.	REUBEN	N.	Last name of the local doctor
X -15.	NYE	O.	___ Killian left home to make his own way
W -16.	POLLY	P.	Billie Jo's last name
L -17.	BAYARD	Q.	The crop Billie Jo's father tried to grow
A -18.	JIM	R.	Miss ___ was Billie Jo's teacher.
C -19.	BUTTERFLY	S.	Billie Jo didn't know how to make ___ sauce.
N -20.	RICE	T.	The funeral of Grandma ___ was important to the Kelbys.
B -21.	POND	U.	The music promoter: ___ Wanderdale
K -22.	ELZIRE	V.	Kind of plant that bloomed at midnight and died at dawn
D -23.	FRANKLIN	W.	Billie Jo's mother: ___ Kelby
M -24.	LIVIE	X.	Last name of Haydon who was an old-time Oklahoman
G -25.	LOUISE	Y.	Arley's wife

Out Of The Dust Magic Squares 1

A. RICE	E. ROMNEY	I. RUSSIAN	M. GUYMON
B. FLOR	F. LUCAS	J. DIONNE	N. POWER
C. POND	G. REUBEN	K. LIVIE	O. HARDLY
D. KELBY	H. VERA	L. FREELAND	P. POPPIES

1. Arley's wife
2. Last name of the local doctor
3. Joe De La ___ was Billie Jo's neighbor.
4. ___ Killian left home to make his own way
5. Last name of the Canadian quintuplets
6. Mr. ___ was the local grocer.
7. What was growing on the graves of soldiers in France
8. Type of thistle Joe De La Flor would feed cattle
9. The Killian daughter Billie Jo was friends with.
10. Billie Jo's father got a job with Wireless ___.
11. Produce deliverer: Pete ___
12. Miss ___ was Billie Jo's teacher.
13. Mr. ___ quarreled about killing rabbits.
14. Billie Jo's last name
15. Billie Jo's mother wanted her husband to dig a ___.
16. The funeral of Grandma ___ was important to the Kelbys.

A=	B=	C=	D=
E=	F=	G=	H=
I=	J=	K=	L=
M=	N=	O=	P=

Out Of The Dust Magic Squares 1 Answer Key

A. RICE
B. FLOR
C. POND
D. KELBY
E. ROMNEY
F. LUCAS
G. REUBEN
H. VERA
I. RUSSIAN
J. DIONNE
K. LIVIE
L. FREELAND
M. GUYMON
N. POWER
O. HARDLY
P. POPPIES

1. Arley's wife
2. Last name of the local doctor
3. Joe De La ___ was Billie Jo's neighbor.
4. ___ Killian left home to make his own way
5. Last name of the Canadian quintuplets
6. Mr. ___ was the local grocer.
7. What was growing on the graves of soldiers in France
8. Type of thistle Joe De La Flor would feed cattle
9. The Killian daughter Billie Jo was friends with.
10. Billie Jo's father got a job with Wireless ___.
11. Produce deliverer: Pete ___
12. Miss ___ was Billie Jo's teacher.
13. Mr. ___ quarreled about killing rabbits.
14. Billie Jo's last name
15. Billie Jo's mother wanted her husband to dig a ___.
16. The funeral of Grandma ___ was important to the Kelbys.

A=2	B=3	C=15	D=14
E=13	F=16	G=4	H=1
I=8	J=5	K=9	L=12
M=11	N=10	O=6	P=7

Out Of The Dust Magic Squares 2

A. NYE
B. ROMNEY
C. BUTTERFLY
D. HARDLY
E. RICE
F. WHEAT
G. CEREUS
H. LUCAS
I. NOBLE
J. JIM
K. ELZIRE
L. FRANKLIN
M. BAYARD
N. CRANBERRY
O. REUBEN
P. FREELAND

1. The funeral of Grandma ___ was important to the Kelbys.
2. Billie Jo's father's last name
3. Mr. ___ quarreled about killing rabbits.
4. First name of the quintuplets' mother
5. The man cleaning up the Crystal Hotel was ___ Martin.
6. The opera Billie Jo didn't know was Madame ___
7. Miss ___ was Billie Jo's teacher.
8. Last name of the local doctor
9. ___ Killian left home to make his own way
10. The crop Billie Jo's father tried to grow
11. Mr. ___ quarreled with Mr. Romney.
12. Mr. ___ was the local grocer.
13. Last name of Haydon who was an old-time Oklahoman
14. Billie Jo's brother who died young
15. Kind of plant that bloomed at midnight and died at dawn
16. Billie Jo didn't know how to make ___ sauce.

A=	B=	C=	D=
E=	F=	G=	H=
I=	J=	K=	L=
M=	N=	O=	P=

Out Of The Dust Magic Squares 2 Answer Key

A. NYE			E. RICE		I. NOBLE	M. BAYARD
B. ROMNEY		F. WHEAT	J. JIM		N. CRANBERRY
C. BUTTERFLY	G. CEREUS	K. ELZIRE	O. REUBEN
D. HARDLY		H. LUCAS	L. FRANKLIN	P. FREELAND

1. The funeral of Grandma ___ was important to the Kelbys.
2. Billie Jo's father's last name
3. Mr. ___ quarreled about killing rabbits.
4. First name of the quintuplets' mother
5. The man cleaning up the Crystal Hotel was ___ Martin.
6. The opera Billie Jo didn't know was Madame ___
7. Miss ___ was Billie Jo's teacher.
8. Last name of the local doctor
9. ___ Killian left home to make his own way
10. The crop Billie Jo's father tried to grow
11. Mr. ___ quarreled with Mr. Romney.
12. Mr. ___ was the local grocer.
13. Last name of Haydon who was an old-time Oklahoman
14. Billie Jo's brother who died young
15. Kind of plant that bloomed at midnight and died at dawn
16. Billie Jo didn't know how to make ___ sauce.

A=13	B=3	C=6	D=12
E=8	F=10	G=15	H=1
I=11	J=5	K=4	L=14
M=2	N=16	O=9	P=7

Out Of The Dust Magic Squares 3

A. HARDLY	E. ELLIE	I. DIONNE	M. POLLY
B. LOUISE	F. POWER	J. BUTTERFLY	N. JIM
C. BAYARD	G. RUSSIAN	K. LIVIE	O. FREELAND
D. POND	H. GUYMON	L. REUBEN	P. NOBLE

1. Billie Jo's mother: ___ Kelby
2. Billie Jo's father got a job with Wireless ___.
3. Produce deliverer: Pete ___
4. Miss ___ was Billie Jo's teacher.
5. ___ Killian left home to make his own way
6. Billie Jo's father's last name
7. Mr. ___ was the local grocer.
8. The opera Billie Jo didn't know was Madame ___
9. The Killian daughter Billie Jo was friends with.
10. Billie Jo's mother wanted her husband to dig a ___.
11. Woman Billie Jo's father got engaged to
12. Last name of the Canadian quintuplets
13. The man cleaning up the Crystal Hotel was ___ Martin.
14. Billie Jo's Aunt ___
15. Type of thistle Joe De La Flor would feed cattle
16. Mr. ___ quarreled with Mr. Romney.

A=	B=	C=	D=
E=	F=	G=	H=
I=	J=	K=	L=
M=	N=	O=	P=

Out Of The Dust Magic Squares 3 Answer Key

A. HARDLY
B. LOUISE
C. BAYARD
D. POND
E. ELLIE
F. POWER
G. RUSSIAN
H. GUYMON
I. DIONNE
J. BUTTERFLY
K. LIVIE
L. REUBEN
M. POLLY
N. JIM
O. FREELAND
P. NOBLE

1. Billie Jo's mother: ___ Kelby
2. Billie Jo's father got a job with Wireless ___.
3. Produce deliverer: Pete ___
4. Miss ___ was Billie Jo's teacher.
5. ___ Killian left home to make his own way
6. Billie Jo's father's last name
7. Mr. ___ was the local grocer.
8. The opera Billie Jo didn't know was Madame ___
9. The Killian daughter Billie Jo was friends with.
10. Billie Jo's mother wanted her husband to dig a ___.
11. Woman Billie Jo's father got engaged to
12. Last name of the Canadian quintuplets
13. The man cleaning up the Crystal Hotel was ___ Martin.
14. Billie Jo's Aunt ___
15. Type of thistle Joe De La Flor would feed cattle
16. Mr. ___ quarreled with Mr. Romney.

A=7	B=11	C=6	D=10
E=14	F=2	G=15	H=3
I=12	J=8	K=9	L=5
M=1	N=13	O=4	P=16

Out Of The Dust Magic Squares 4

A. ELLIE
B. FREELAND
C. LOUISE
D. ARLEY
E. POND
F. NOBLE
G. DIONNE
H. NYE
I. POPPIES
J. POWER
K. JIM
L. LIVIE
M. FLOR
N. ELZIRE
O. CRADDOCK
P. BUTTERFLY

1. Miss ___ was Billie Jo's teacher.
2. Last name of the Canadian quintuplets
3. The man cleaning up the Crystal Hotel was ___ Martin.
4. First name of the quintuplets' mother
5. Joe De La ___ was Billie Jo's neighbor.
6. The Killian daughter Billie Jo was friends with.
7. Last name of Haydon who was an old-time Oklahoman
8. Billie Jo's Aunt ___
9. The opera Billie Jo didn't know was Madame ___
10. What was growing on the graves of soldiers in France
11. Billie Jo's mother wanted her husband to dig a ___.
12. The music promoter: ___ Wanderdale
13. Woman Billie Jo's father got engaged to
14. Mr. ___ quarreled with Mr. Romney.
15. Billie Jo's father got a job with Wireless ___.
16. Mad Dog's last name

A=	B=	C=	D=
E=	F=	G=	H=
I=	J=	K=	L=
M=	N=	O=	P=

Out Of The Dust Magic Squares 4 Answer Key

A. ELLIE	E. POND	I. POPPIES	M. FLOR
B. FREELAND	F. NOBLE	J. POWER	N. ELZIRE
C. LOUISE	G. DIONNE	K. JIM	O. CRADDOCK
D. ARLEY	H. NYE	L. LIVIE	P. BUTTERFLY

1. Miss ___ was Billie Jo's teacher.
2. Last name of the Canadian quintuplets
3. The man cleaning up the Crystal Hotel was ___ Martin.
4. First name of the quintuplets' mother
5. Joe De La ___ was Billie Jo's neighbor.
6. The Killian daughter Billie Jo was friends with.
7. Last name of Haydon who was an old-time Oklahoman
8. Billie Jo's Aunt ___
9. The opera Billie Jo didn't know was Madame ___
10. What was growing on the graves of soldiers in France
11. Billie Jo's mother wanted her husband to dig a ___.
12. The music promoter: ___ Wanderdale
13. Woman Billie Jo's father got engaged to
14. Mr. ___ quarreled with Mr. Romney.
15. Billie Jo's father got a job with Wireless ___.
16. Mad Dog's last name

A=8	B=1	C=13	D=12
E=11	F=14	G=2	H=7
I=10	J=15	K=3	L=6
M=5	N=4	O=16	P=9

Out Of The Dust Word Search 1

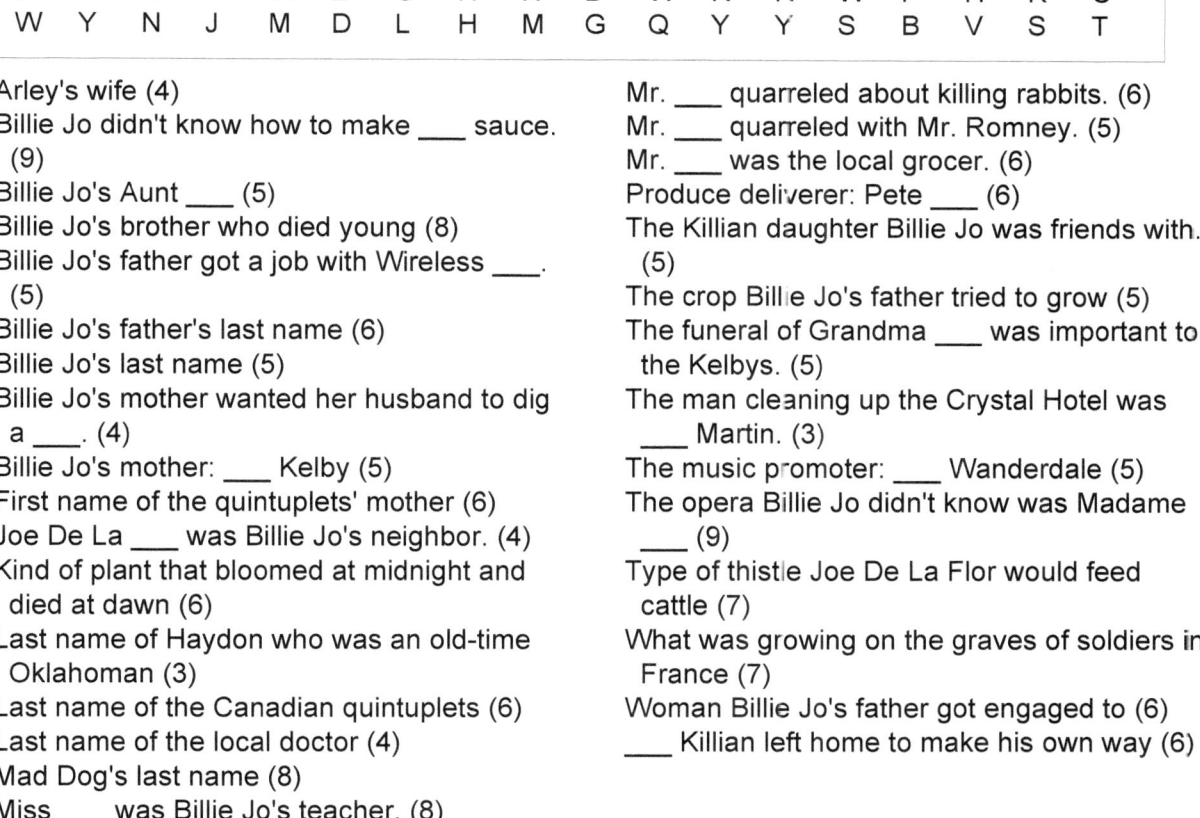

Arley's wife (4)
Billie Jo didn't know how to make ___ sauce. (9)
Billie Jo's Aunt ___ (5)
Billie Jo's brother who died young (8)
Billie Jo's father got a job with Wireless ___. (5)
Billie Jo's father's last name (6)
Billie Jo's last name (5)
Billie Jo's mother wanted her husband to dig a ___. (4)
Billie Jo's mother: ___ Kelby (5)
First name of the quintuplets' mother (6)
Joe De La ___ was Billie Jo's neighbor. (4)
Kind of plant that bloomed at midnight and died at dawn (6)
Last name of Haydon who was an old-time Oklahoman (3)
Last name of the Canadian quintuplets (6)
Last name of the local doctor (4)
Mad Dog's last name (8)
Miss ___ was Billie Jo's teacher. (8)

Mr. ___ quarreled about killing rabbits. (6)
Mr. ___ quarreled with Mr. Romney. (5)
Mr. ___ was the local grocer. (6)
Produce deliverer: Pete ___ (6)
The Killian daughter Billie Jo was friends with. (5)
The crop Billie Jo's father tried to grow (5)
The funeral of Grandma ___ was important to the Kelbys. (5)
The man cleaning up the Crystal Hotel was ___ Martin. (3)
The music promoter: ___ Wanderdale (5)
The opera Billie Jo didn't know was Madame ___ (9)
Type of thistle Joe De La Flor would feed cattle (7)
What was growing on the graves of soldiers in France (7)
Woman Billie Jo's father got engaged to (6)
___ Killian left home to make his own way (6)

Out Of The Dust Word Search 1 Answer Key

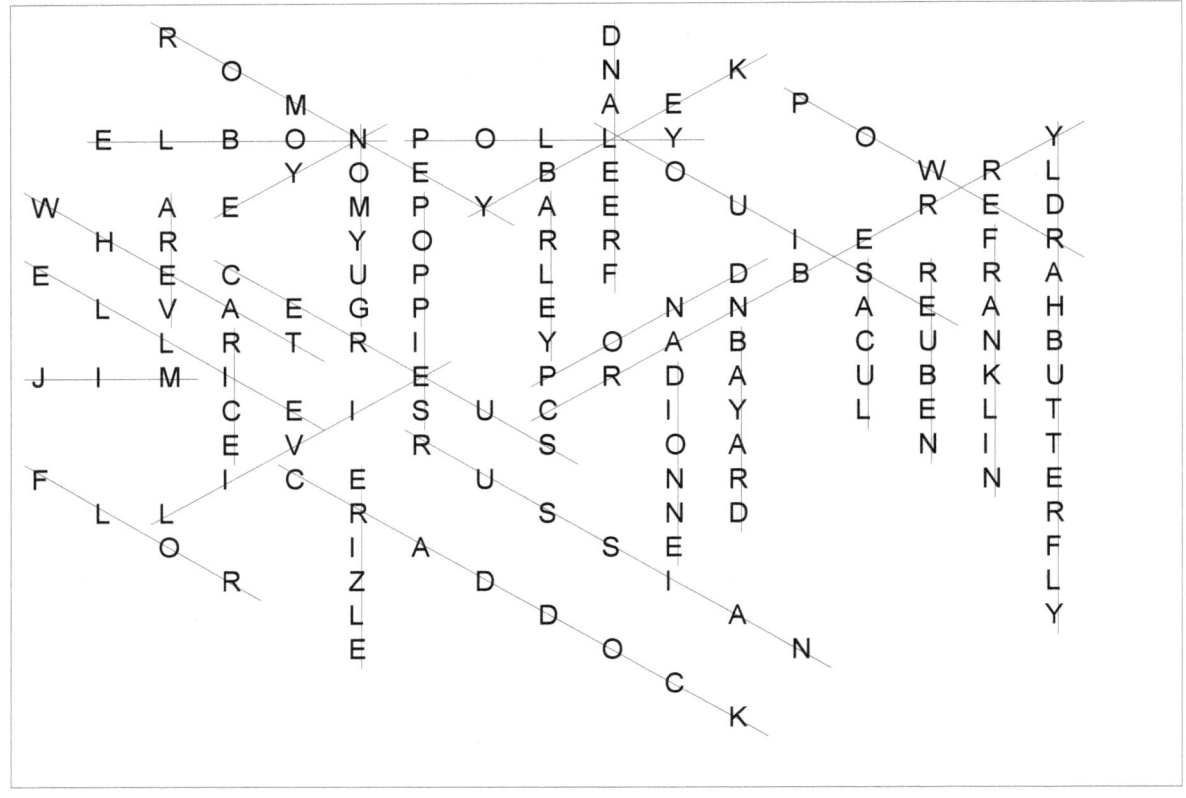

Arley's wife (4)
Billie Jo didn't know how to make ___ sauce. (9)
Billie Jo's Aunt ___ (5)
Billie Jo's brother who died young (8)
Billie Jo's father got a job with Wireless ___. (5)
Billie Jo's father's last name (6)
Billie Jo's last name (5)
Billie Jo's mother wanted her husband to dig a ___. (4)
Billie Jo's mother: ___ Kelby (5)
First name of the quintuplets' mother (6)
Joe De La ___ was Billie Jo's neighbor. (4)
Kind of plant that bloomed at midnight and died at dawn (6)
Last name of Haydon who was an old-time Oklahoman (3)
Last name of the Canadian quintuplets (6)
Last name of the local doctor (4)
Mad Dog's last name (8)
Miss ___ was Billie Jo's teacher. (8)

Mr. ___ quarreled about killing rabbits. (6)
Mr. ___ quarreled with Mr. Romney. (5)
Mr. ___ was the local grocer. (6)
Produce deliverer: Pete ___ (6)
The Killian daughter Billie Jo was friends with. (5)
The crop Billie Jo's father tried to grow (5)
The funeral of Grandma ___ was important to the Kelbys. (5)
The man cleaning up the Crystal Hotel was ___ Martin. (3)
The music promoter: ___ Wanderdale (5)
The opera Billie Jo didn't know was Madame ___ (9)
Type of thistle Joe De La Flor would feed cattle (7)
What was growing on the graves of soldiers in France (7)
Woman Billie Jo's father got engaged to (6)
___ Killian left home to make his own way (6)

Out Of The Dust Word Search 2

Arley's wife (4)
Billie Jo didn't know how to make ___ sauce. (9)
Billie Jo's Aunt ___ (5)
Billie Jo's brother who died young (8)
Billie Jo's father got a job with Wireless ___. (5)
Billie Jo's father's last name (6)
Billie Jo's last name (5)
Billie Jo's mother wanted her husband to dig a ___. (4)
Billie Jo's mother: ___ Kelby (5)
First name of the quintuplets' mother (6)
Joe De La ___ was Billie Jo's neighbor. (4)
Kind of plant that bloomed at midnight and died at dawn (6)
Last name of Haydon who was an old-time Oklahoman (3)
Last name of the Canadian quintuplets (6)
Last name of the local doctor (4)
Mad Dog's last name (8)
Miss ___ was Billie Jo's teacher. (8)
Mr. ___ quarreled about killing rabbits. (6)
Mr. ___ quarreled with Mr. Romney. (5)
Mr. ___ was the local grocer. (6)
Produce deliverer: Pete ___ (6)
The Killian daughter Billie Jo was friends with. (5)
The crop Billie Jo's father tried to grow (5)
The funeral of Grandma ___ was important to the Kelbys. (5)
The man cleaning up the Crystal Hotel was ___ Martin. (3)
The music promoter: ___ Wanderdale (5)
The opera Billie Jo didn't know was Madame ___ (9)
Type of thistle Joe De La Flor would feed cattle (7)
What was growing on the graves of soldiers in France (7)
Woman Billie Jo's father got engaged to (6)
___ Killian left home to make his own way (6)

Out Of The Dust Word Search 2 Answer Key

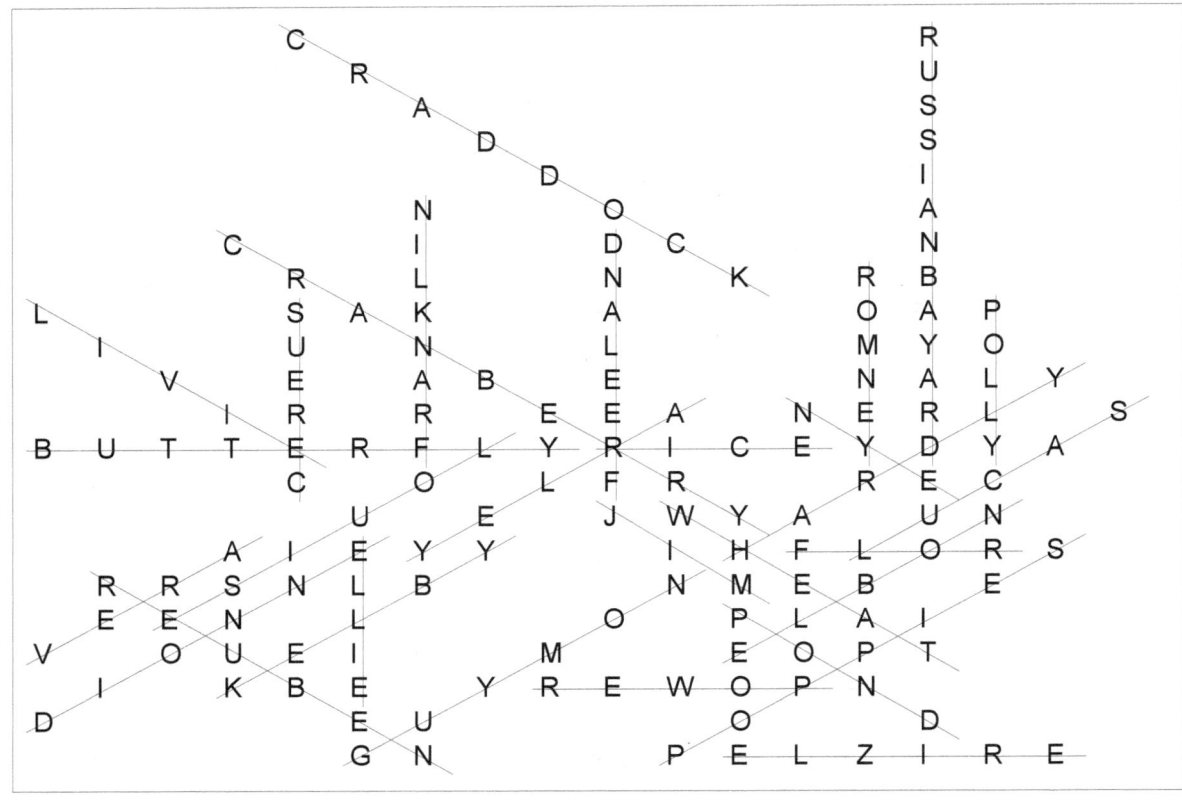

Arley's wife (4)
Billie Jo didn't know how to make ___ sauce. (9)
Billie Jo's Aunt ___ (5)
Billie Jo's brother who died young (8)
Billie Jo's father got a job with Wireless ___. (5)
Billie Jo's father's last name (6)
Billie Jo's last name (5)
Billie Jo's mother wanted her husband to dig a ___. (4)
Billie Jo's mother: ___ Kelby (5)
First name of the quintuplets' mother (6)
Joe De La ___ was Billie Jo's neighbor. (4)
Kind of plant that bloomed at midnight and died at dawn (6)
Last name of Haydon who was an old-time Oklahoman (3)
Last name of the Canadian quintuplets (6)
Last name of the local doctor (4)
Mad Dog's last name (8)
Miss ___ was Billie Jo's teacher. (8)

Mr. ___ quarreled about killing rabbits. (6)
Mr. ___ quarreled with Mr. Romney. (5)
Mr. ___ was the local grocer. (6)
Produce deliverer: Pete ___ (6)
The Killian daughter Billie Jo was friends with. (5)
The crop Billie Jo's father tried to grow (5)
The funeral of Grandma ___ was important to the Kelbys. (5)
The man cleaning up the Crystal Hotel was ___ Martin. (3)
The music promoter: ___ Wanderdale (5)
The opera Billie Jo didn't know was Madame ___ (9)
Type of thistle Joe De La Flor would feed cattle (7)
What was growing on the graves of soldiers in France (7)
Woman Billie Jo's father got engaged to (6)
___ Killian left home to make his own way (6)

Out Of The Dust Word Search 3

```
E L L I E S E I P P O P E P O L L Y
R Y Q O U C C L C V M Y Z B I F U S
H B V E U N R B Z T N S J V D R C B
C L R F C I R A D I Y T I D V E A Q
N E Q Z N L S B N S R E R I C E S Y
C K C K W K W E O B X E K S X L X J
Q B R K T N Q H P V E T H T B A G P
N J A N V A W L X Y R R A V G N M Y
L I D Y C R R C E Z U R R K T D N T
N M D N A F Z N M S E B H Y T R Y D
H Q O S V R M P S V H C W K G H P J
C S C Q D O D I N M Y S C L B R Y V
D S K N R K A N C F N R J V U X F G
D L G B V N T W N S L G B R T N B J
B N N R P R M M E N S U S Z T N T J
Q K B G B O D T B G D Y V G E X F K
R G T F B F W T U G K M A E R H B J
B R N P S Q R E E W T O N R F F C K
R R G N Y Y L D R A H N O B L E W T
D L H M Q M X Z E H O Y F O Y E Q X
V D L P K Q D H S I D C R P V R Y L
P Q B M X H W V D H B T K G H V T L
```

ARLEY	ELLIE	JIM	POLLY	RUSSIAN
BAYARD	ELZIRE	KELBY	POND	VERA
BUTTERFLY	FLOR	LIVIE	POPPIES	WHEAT
CEREUS	FRANKLIN	LOUISE	POWER	
CRADDOCK	FREELAND	LUCAS	REUBEN	
CRANBERRY	GUYMON	NOBLE	RICE	
DIONNE	HARDLY	NYE	ROMNEY	

Out Of The Dust Word Search 3 Answer Key

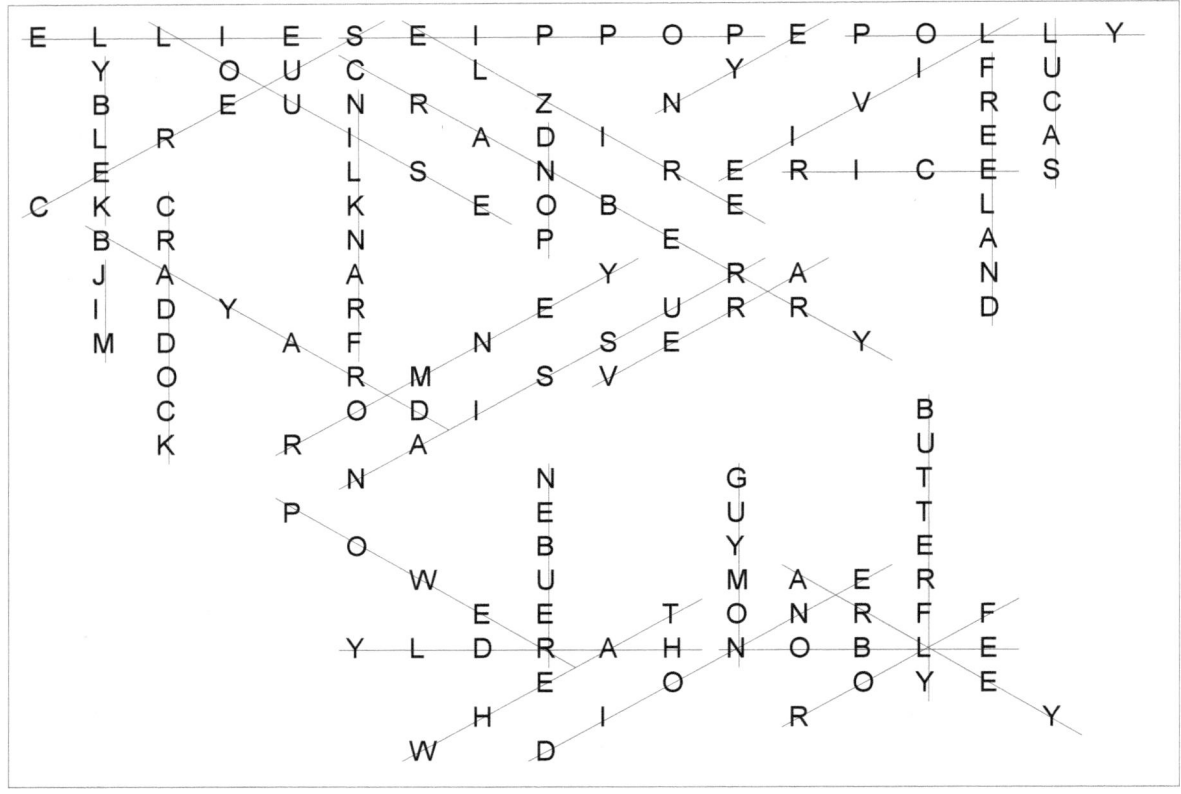

ARLEY	ELLIE	JIM	POLLY	RUSSIAN
BAYARD	ELZIRE	KELBY	POND	VERA
BUTTERFLY	FLOR	LIVIE	POPPIES	WHEAT
CEREUS	FRANKLIN	LOUISE	POWER	
CRADDOCK	FREELAND	LUCAS	REUBEN	
CRANBERRY	GUYMON	NOBLE	RICE	
DIONNE	HARDLY	NYE	ROMNEY	

Out Of The Dust Word Search 4

```
Z Y Q C R A N B E R R Y J T S J T S
Q J P J M G J C B C W Y B Z T W X T
D L P F H G B G G R W R F W B F Y J
H G C P L M R V N A Q Z N L H J D K
P R F N Y X Q W G D K X N F P P I T
X D X D P X F N R D Y R M O D S O H
L V H P C H R B T O E E S G B M N Q
T D A H F L F C L C N R L Q B L N F
Z F R N N Y B L E K M C U Z A R E V
G N D W N N G Q Z I O X C S I I Z G
B U L E H N W R J H R Q A E V R B K
U L Y F R E E L A N D L S I F C E T
T N L M P W A J R I N T L P L E L W
T J L C O Z B T L L O Q R P S R L Z
E K O P P N Q A E K P G U O J E I Z
R C P L F R Y N Y N J C S P R U E F
F N T O C L K M P A W H S F I S H P
L D Y U S L O W M R R M I V C W R X
Y D Y I L L H R Y F R D A Z E P F D
C F P S T K J T Y B X L N R Y K S Z
N X B E T G N T P Y K J L Y D Y S P
G M S C S J R E U B E N W N Y X T Y
```

ARLEY	ELLIE	JIM	POLLY	RUSSIAN
BAYARD	ELZIRE	KELBY	POND	VERA
BUTTERFLY	FLOR	LIVIE	POPPIES	WHEAT
CEREUS	FRANKLIN	LOUISE	POWER	
CRADDOCK	FREELAND	LUCAS	REUBEN	
CRANBERRY	GUYMON	NOBLE	RICE	
DIONNE	HARDLY	NYE	ROMNEY	

Out Of The Dust Word Search 4 Answer Key

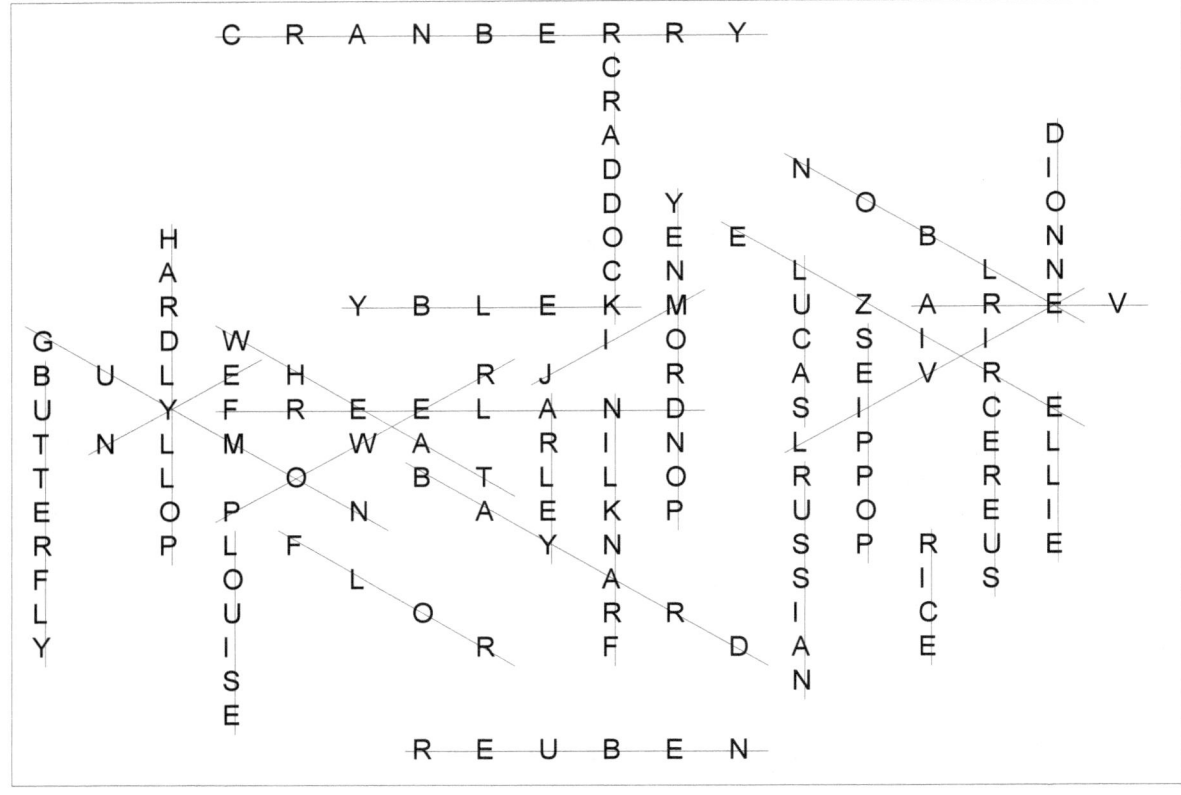

ARLEY	ELLIE	JIM	POLLY	RUSSIAN
BAYARD	ELZIRE	KELBY	POND	VERA
BUTTERFLY	FLOR	LIVIE	POPPIES	WHEAT
CEREUS	FRANKLIN	LOUISE	POWER	
CRADDOCK	FREELAND	LUCAS	REUBEN	
CRANBERRY	GUYMON	NOBLE	RICE	
DIONNE	HARDLY	NYE	ROMNEY	

Out Of The Dust Crossword 1

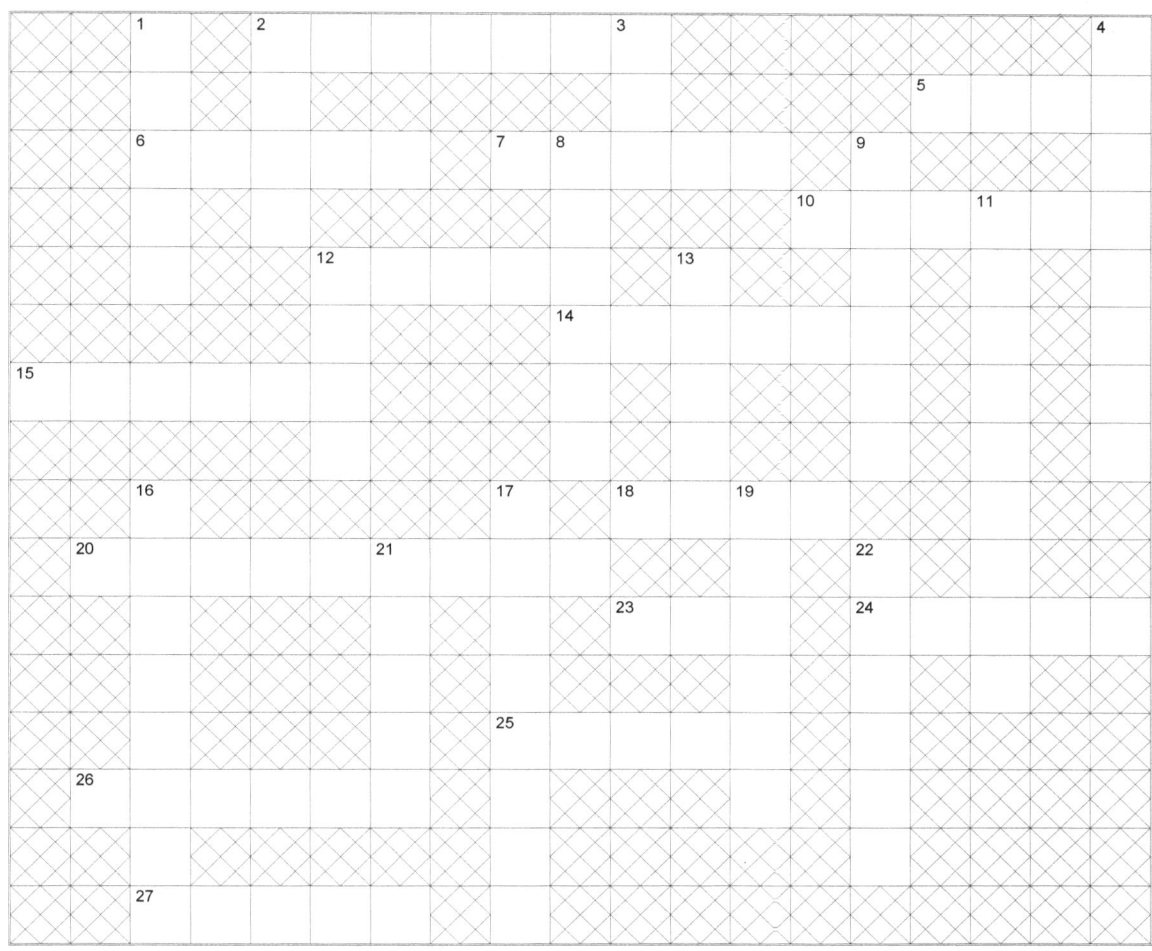

Across
2. Type of thistle Joe De La Flor would feed cattle
5. Joe De La ___ was Billie Jo's neighbor.
6. The funeral of Grandma ___ was important to the Kelbys.
7. The crop Billie Jo's father tried to grow
10. ___ Killian left home to make his own way
12. Billie Jo's father got a job with Wireless ___.
14. Last name of the Canadian quintuplets
15. Produce deliverer: Pete ___
18. Arley's wife
20. Billie Jo didn't know how to make ___ sauce.
23. The man cleaning up the Crystal Hotel was ___ Martin.
24. The music promoter: ___ Wanderdale
25. The Killian daughter Billie Jo was friends with.
26. Woman Billie Jo's father got engaged to
27. Billie Jo's last name

Down
1. Billie Jo's mother: ___ Kelby
2. Last name of the local doctor
3. Last name of Haydon who was an old-time Oklahoman
4. Billie Jo's brother who died young
8. Mr. ___ was the local grocer.
9. Kind of plant that bloomed at midnight and died at dawn
11. The opera Billie Jo didn't know was Madame ___
12. Billie Jo's mother wanted her husband to dig a ___.
13. Mr. ___ quarreled with Mr. Romney.
16. Mad Dog's last name
17. Miss ___ was Billie Jo's teacher.
19. Mr. ___ quarreled about killing rabbits.
21. Billie Jo's Aunt ___
22. Billie Jo's father's last name

Out Of The Dust Crossword 1 Answer Key

	1 P	2 R	U	S	S	I	3 A	N				4 F
	O		I				Y			5 F	L	O	R
	6 L	U	C	A	S		7 W	8 H	E	A	T		9 C			A
	L		E					A				10 R	E	11 U	B	E	N
	Y		12 P	O	W	E	R		13 N		R		U		K
			O			14 D	I	O	N	N	E		T		L
15 G	U	Y	M	O	N		L		B		U		T		I
			D				Y		L		S		E		N
		16 C			17 F		18 V	E	19 R	A			R		
	20 C	R	A	N	B	21 E	R	R	Y			22 B		F	
		A				L				23 J	I	M		24 A	R	L	E	Y
		D				L					N		Y		Y
		D				I		25 L	I	V	I	E		A
	26 L	O	U	I	S	E		A				Y		R
		C						N					D
		27 K	E	L	B	Y		D				

Across

2. Type of thistle Joe De La Flor would feed cattle
5. Joe De La ___ was Billie Jo's neighbor.
6. The funeral of Grandma ___ was important to the Kelbys.
7. The crop Billie Jo's father tried to grow
10. ___ Killian left home to make his own way
12. Billie Jo's father got a job with Wireless ___.
14. Last name of the Canadian quintuplets
15. Produce deliverer: Pete ___
18. Arley's wife
20. Billie Jo didn't know how to make ___ sauce.
23. The man cleaning up the Crystal Hotel was ___ Martin.
24. The music promoter: ___ Wanderdale
25. The Killian daughter Billie Jo was friends with.
26. Woman Billie Jo's father got engaged to
27. Billie Jo's last name

Down

1. Billie Jo's mother: ___ Kelby
2. Last name of the local doctor
3. Last name of Haydon who was an old-time Oklahoman
4. Billie Jo's brother who died young
8. Mr. ___ was the local grocer.
9. Kind of plant that bloomed at midnight and died at dawn
11. The opera Billie Jo didn't know was Madame ___
12. Billie Jo's mother wanted her husband to dig a ___.
13. Mr. ___ quarreled with Mr. Romney.
16. Mad Dog's last name
17. Miss ___ was Billie Jo's teacher.
19. Mr. ___ quarreled about killing rabbits.
21. Billie Jo's Aunt ___
22. Billie Jo's father's last name

Out Of The Dust Crossword 2

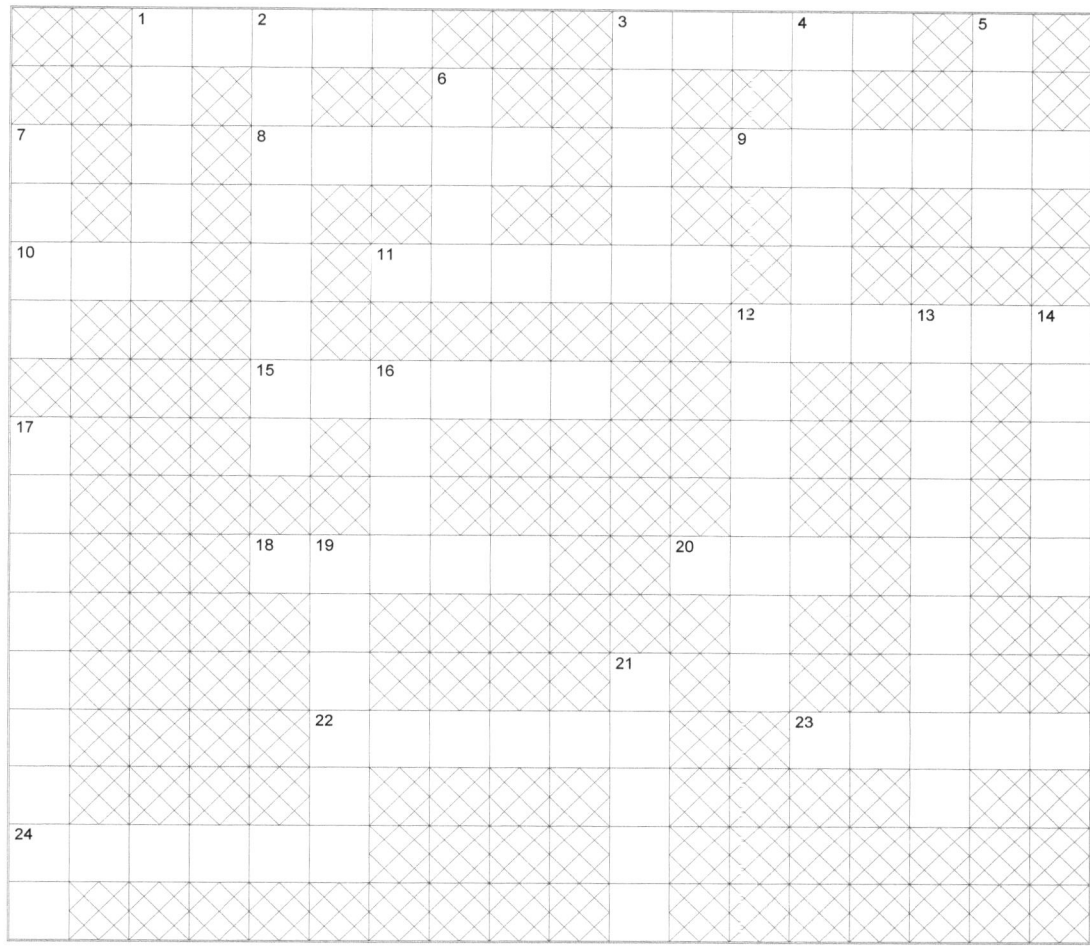

Across
1. The funeral of Grandma ___ was important to the Kelbys.
3. Billie Jo's mother: ___ Kelby
8. The music promoter: ___ Wanderdale
9. Produce deliverer: Pete ___
10. Last name of Haydon who was an old-time Oklahoman
11. Billie Jo's father's last name
12. ___ Killian left home to make his own way
15. Kind of plant that bloomed at midnight and died at dawn
18. The crop Billie Jo's father tried to grow
20. The man cleaning up the Crystal Hotel was ___ Martin.
22. Last name of the Canadian quintuplets
23. Billie Jo's Aunt ___
24. Mr. ___ quarreled about killing rabbits.

Down
1. The Killian daughter Billie Jo was friends with.
2. Mad Dog's last name
3. Billie Jo's father got a job with Wireless ___.
4. Woman Billie Jo's father got engaged to
5. Joe De La ___ was Billie Jo's neighbor.
6. Arley's wife
7. Billie Jo's mother wanted her husband to dig a ___.
12. Type of thistle Joe De La Flor would feed cattle
13. The opera Billie Jo didn't know was Madame ___
14. Mr. ___ quarreled with Mr. Romney.
16. Last name of the local doctor
17. Billie Jo didn't know how to make ___ sauce.
19. Mr. ___ was the local grocer.
21. Billie Jo's last name

Out Of The Dust Crossword 2 Answer Key

		1 L	2 C	A	S			3 P	4 O	L	L	Y	5 F	
		I		R		6 V		O		O			L	
7 P		V	8 A	R	L	E	Y		9 W		G	U	Y	M	O	N
O		I	D			R			E		I		R	
10 N	Y	E	D		11 B	A	Y	A	R	D		S		
D			O							12 R	E	U	13 B	E	14 N
		15 C	E	16 R	E	U	S			U			U		O
17 C		K		I						S			T		B
R				C						S			T		L
A		18 W	19 H	E	A	T			20 J	I	M		E		E
N			A						A				R		
B			R					21 K		N			F		
E		22 D	I	O	N	N	E			23 E	L	L	I	E
R			L					L					Y	
24 R	O	M	N	E	Y			B						
Y								Y						

Across
1. The funeral of Grandma ___ was important to the Kelbys.
3. Billie Jo's mother: ___ Kelby
8. The music promoter: ___ Wanderdale
9. Produce deliverer: Pete ___
10. Last name of Haydon who was an old-time Oklahoman
11. Billie Jo's father's last name
12. ___ Killian left home to make his own way
15. Kind of plant that bloomed at midnight and died at dawn
18. The crop Billie Jo's father tried to grow
20. The man cleaning up the Crystal Hotel was ___ Martin.
22. Last name of the Canadian quintuplets
23. Billie Jo's Aunt ___
24. Mr. ___ quarreled about killing rabbits.

Down
1. The Killian daughter Billie Jo was friends with.
2. Mad Dog's last name
3. Billie Jo's father got a job with Wireless ___.
4. Woman Billie Jo's father got engaged to
5. Joe De La ___ was Billie Jo's neighbor.
6. Arley's wife
7. Billie Jo's mother wanted her husband to dig a ___.
12. Type of thistle Joe De La Flor would feed cattle
13. The opera Billie Jo didn't know was Madame ___
14. Mr. ___ quarreled with Mr. Romney.
16. Last name of the local doctor
17. Billie Jo didn't know how to make ___ sauce.
19. Mr. ___ was the local grocer.
21. Billie Jo's last name

Out Of The Dust Crossword 3

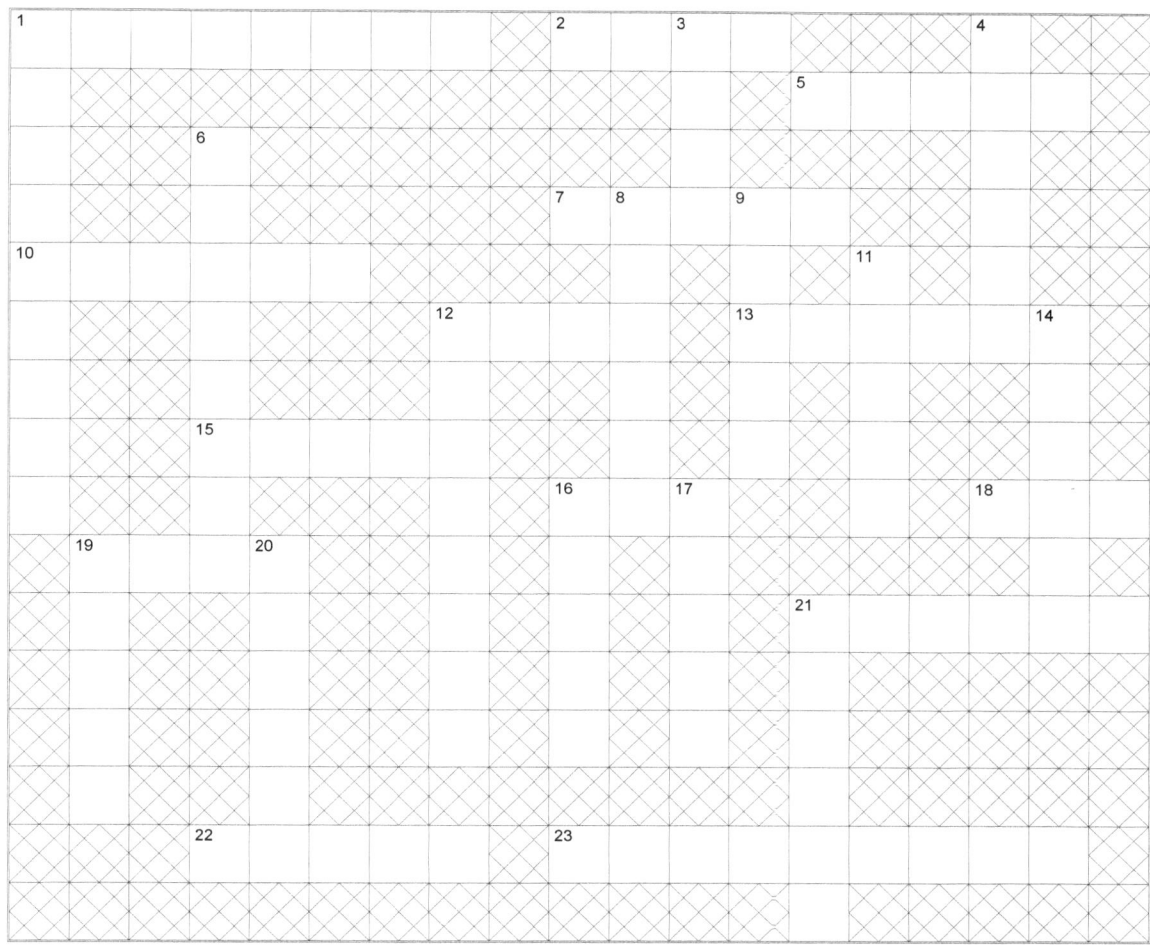

Across
1. Mad Dog's last name
2. Arley's wife
5. Billie Jo's father got a job with Wireless ___.
7. The crop Billie Jo's father tried to grow
10. Billie Jo's father's last name
12. Joe De La ___ was Billie Jo's neighbor.
13. Woman Billie Jo's father got engaged to
15. The Killian daughter Billie Jo was friends with.
16. Last name of Haydon who was an old-time Oklahoman
18. The man cleaning up the Crystal Hotel was ___ Martin.
19. Billie Jo's mother wanted her husband to dig a ___.
21. Mr. ___ quarreled about killing rabbits.
22. Billie Jo's last name
23. The opera Billie Jo didn't know was Madame ___

Down
1. Billie Jo didn't know how to make ___ sauce.
3. Last name of the local doctor
4. Kind of plant that bloomed at midnight and died at dawn
6. Billie Jo's brother who died young
8. Mr. ___ was the local grocer.
9. The music promoter: ___ Wanderdale
11. The funeral of Grandma ___ was important to the Kelbys.
12. Miss ___ was Billie Jo's teacher.
14. First name of the quintuplets' mother
16. Mr. ___ quarreled with Mr. Romney.
17. Billie Jo's Aunt ___
19. Billie Jo's mother: ___ Kelby
20. Last name of the Canadian quintuplets
21. ___ Killian left home to make his own way

Out Of The Dust Crossword 3 Answer Key

	1 C	R	A	D	D	O	C	K		2 V	3 E	R	A		4 C	
	R									I		5 P	O	W	E	R
	A			6 F							C				R	
	N			R			7 W	8 H	9 E	A	T				E	
10 B	A	Y	A	R	D			A	R			11 L		U		
E				A	N		12 F	L	O	R		13 L	O	U	I	S	E
R				K			R		D		E		C		L	
R			15 L	I	V	I	E		L		Y		A		Z	
Y			I				E		16 N	17 Y	E		S		18 J	I	M
	19 P	O	N	20 D			L		O		L				R	
	O			I			A		B		L		21 R	O	M	N	E	Y
	L			O			N		L		I		E			
	L			N			D		E		E		U			
	Y			N									B			
		22 K	E	L	B	Y		23 B	U	T	T	E	R	F	L	Y
								N							

Across
1. Mad Dog's last name
2. Arley's wife
5. Billie Jo's father got a job with Wireless ___.
7. The crop Billie Jo's father tried to grow
10. Billie Jo's father's last name
12. Joe De La ___ was Billie Jo's neighbor.
13. Woman Billie Jo's father got engaged to
15. The Killian daughter Billie Jo was friends with.
16. Last name of Haydon who was an old-time Oklahoman
18. The man cleaning up the Crystal Hotel was ___ Martin.
19. Billie Jo's mother wanted her husband to dig a ___.
21. Mr. ___ quarreled about killing rabbits.
22. Billie Jo's last name
23. The opera Billie Jo didn't know was Madame ___

Down
1. Billie Jo didn't know how to make ___ sauce.
3. Last name of the local doctor
4. Kind of plant that bloomed at midnight and died at dawn
6. Billie Jo's brother who died young
8. Mr. ___ was the local grocer.
9. The music promoter: ___ Wanderdale
11. The funeral of Grandma ___ was important to the Kelbys.
12. Miss ___ was Billie Jo's teacher.
14. First name of the quintuplets' mother
16. Mr. ___ quarreled with Mr. Romney.
17. Billie Jo's Aunt ___
19. Billie Jo's mother: ___ Kelby
20. Last name of the Canadian quintuplets
21. ___ Killian left home to make his own way

Out Of The Dust Crossword 4

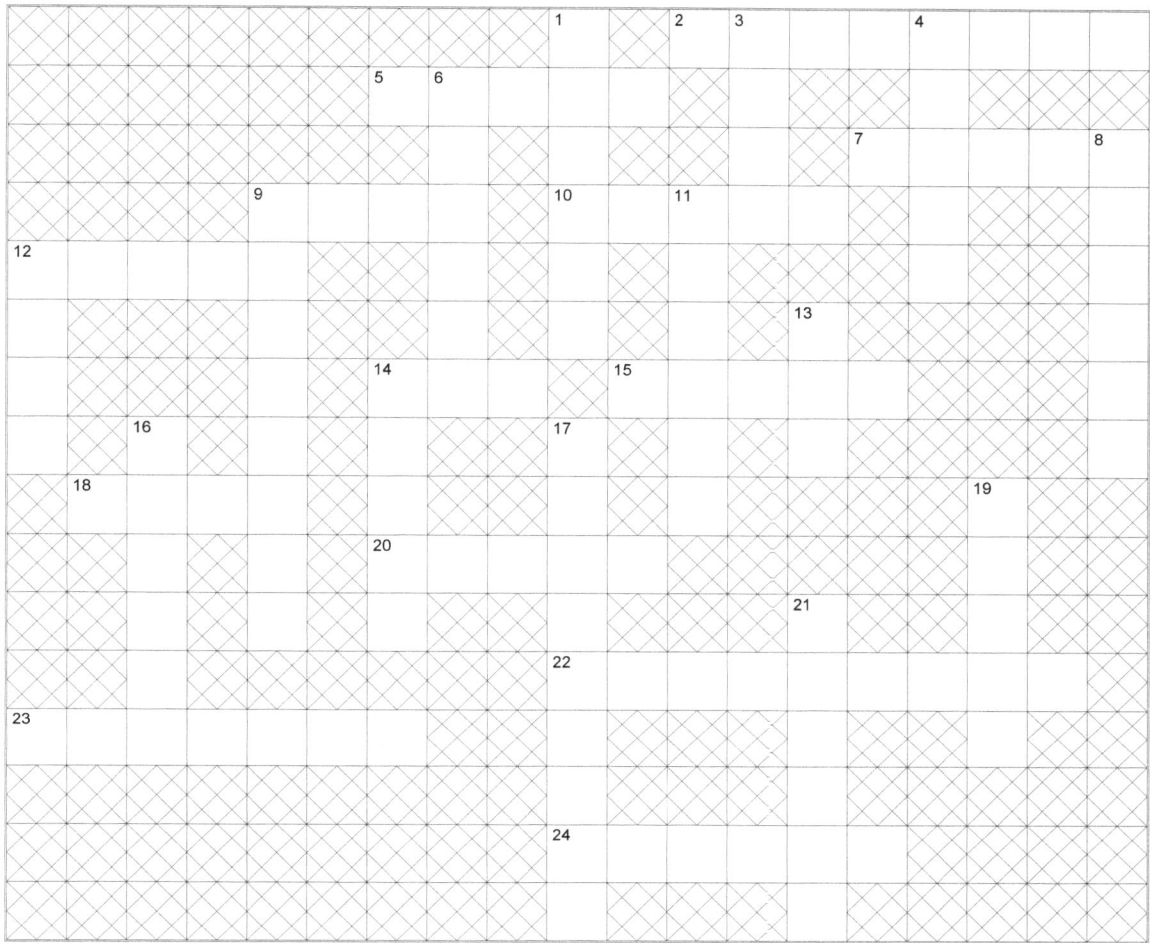

Across
2. Billie Jo's brother who died young
5. The crop Billie Jo's father tried to grow
7. Billie Jo's Aunt ___
9. Joe De La ___ was Billie Jo's neighbor.
10. The music promoter: ___ Wanderdale
12. Billie Jo's father got a job with Wireless ___.
14. Last name of Haydon who was an old-time Oklahoman
15. The Killian daughter Billie Jo was friends with.
18. Arley's wife
20. The funeral of Grandma ___ was important to the Kelbys.
22. The opera Billie Jo didn't know was Madame ___
23. Type of thistle Joe De La Flor would feed cattle
24. Mr. ___ quarreled about killing rabbits.

Down
1. Billie Jo's father's last name
3. Last name of the local doctor
4. Billie Jo's last name
6. Mr. ___ was the local grocer.
8. First name of the quintuplets' mother
9. Miss ___ was Billie Jo's teacher.
11. Woman Billie Jo's father got engaged to
12. Billie Jo's mother wanted her husband to dig a ___.
13. The man cleaning up the Crystal Hotel was ___ Martin.
14. Mr. ___ quarreled with Mr. Romney.
16. Kind of plant that bloomed at midnight and died at dawn
17. Billie Jo didn't know how to make ___ sauce.
19. Billie Jo's mother: ___ Kelby
21. ___ Killian left home to make his own way

Out Of The Dust Crossword 4 Answer Key

							1 B		2 F	3 R	A	N	4 K	L	I	N
				5 W	6 H	E	A	T		I			E			
					A		Y			C		7 E	L	L	I	8 E
			9 F	L	O	R		10 A	11 R	L	E	Y		B		L
12 P	O	W	E	R				D		R				Y		Z
O			E					L		D		13 J				I
N			E			14 N	Y	E		15 L	I	V	I	E		R
D		16 C	L			O			17 C		S	M			19 P	E
	18 V	E	R	A		B			R		E				O	
		R		N		20 L	U	C	A	S			21 R		L	
		E		D		E			N				R		L	
		U						22 B	U	T	T	E	R	F	L	Y
23 R	U	S	S	I	A	N		E			U			Y		
								R			B					
								24 R	O	M	N	E	Y			
								Y			N					

Across
2. Billie Jo's brother who died young
5. The crop Billie Jo's father tried to grow
7. Billie Jo's Aunt ___
9. Joe De La ___ was Billie Jo's neighbor.
10. The music promoter: ___ Wanderdale
12. Billie Jo's father got a job with Wireless ___.
14. Last name of Haydon who was an old-time Oklahoman
15. The Killian daughter Billie Jo was friends with.
18. Arley's wife
20. The funeral of Grandma ___ was important to the Kelbys.
22. The opera Billie Jo didn't know was Madame ___
23. Type of thistle Joe De La Flor would feed cattle
24. Mr. ___ quarreled about killing rabbits.

Down
1. Billie Jo's father's last name
3. Last name of the local doctor
4. Billie Jo's last name
6. Mr. ___ was the local grocer.
8. First name of the quintuplets' mother
9. Miss ___ was Billie Jo's teacher.
11. Woman Billie Jo's father got engaged to
12. Billie Jo's mother wanted her husband to dig a ___.
13. The man cleaning up the Crystal Hotel was ___ Martin.
14. Mr. ___ quarreled with Mr. Romney.
16. Kind of plant that bloomed at midnight and died at dawn
17. Billie Jo didn't know how to make ___ sauce.
19. Billie Jo's mother: ___ Kelby
21. ___ Killian left home to make his own way

Out Of The Dust

VERA	FLOR	FREELAND	WHEAT	CRADDOCK
ROMNEY	CEREUS	RICE	LIVIE	NOBLE
LUCAS	CRANBERRY	FREE SPACE	ELLIE	POND
POLLY	REUBEN	RUSSIAN	LOUISE	GUYMON
FRANKLIN	KELBY	NYE	POPPIES	BAYARD

Out Of The Dust

ELZIRE	HARDLY	DIONNE	POWER	JIM
ARLEY	BAYARD	POPPIES	NYE	KELBY
FRANKLIN	GUYMON	FREE SPACE	RUSSIAN	REUBEN
POLLY	POND	ELLIE	BUTTERFLY	CRANBERRY
LUCAS	NOBLE	LIVIE	RICE	CEREUS

Out Of The Dust

CRADDOCK	POWER	BAYARD	ARLEY	FRANKLIN
VERA	ELLIE	GUYMON	RUSSIAN	WHEAT
KELBY	HARDLY	FREE SPACE	NYE	DIONNE
JIM	ELZIRE	ROMNEY	BUTTERFLY	CEREUS
POPPIES	CRANBERRY	RICE	LUCAS	REUBEN

Out Of The Dust

NOBLE	LIVIE	LOUISE	POLLY	POND
FLOR	REUBEN	LUCAS	RICE	CRANBERRY
POPPIES	CEREUS	FREE SPACE	ROMNEY	ELZIRE
JIM	DIONNE	NYE	FREELAND	HARDLY
KELBY	WHEAT	RUSSIAN	GUYMON	ELLIE

Out Of The Dust

LOUISE	VERA	FRANKLIN	HARDLY	POWER
LUCAS	ARLEY	RUSSIAN	CRANBERRY	REUBEN
GUYMON	POLLY	FREE SPACE	POPPIES	NYE
WHEAT	ROMNEY	CEREUS	BAYARD	KELBY
JIM	BUTTERFLY	DIONNE	CRADDOCK	FREELAND

Out Of The Dust

POND	ELZIRE	LIVIE	ELLIE	NOBLE
RICE	FREELAND	CRADDOCK	DIONNE	BUTTERFLY
JIM	KELBY	FREE SPACE	CEREUS	ROMNEY
WHEAT	NYE	POPPIES	FLOR	POLLY
GUYMON	REUBEN	CRANBERRY	RUSSIAN	ARLEY

Out Of The Dust

KELBY	CEREUS	NYE	FLOR	BAYARD
LIVIE	POWER	LUCAS	HARDLY	JIM
POND	ELZIRE	FREE SPACE	CRANBERRY	GUYMON
DIONNE	FREELAND	LOUISE	ARLEY	BUTTERFLY
RUSSIAN	POLLY	CRADDOCK	ELLIE	POPPIES

Out Of The Dust

REUBEN	VERA	ROMNEY	WHEAT	FRANKLIN
RICE	POPPIES	ELLIE	CRADDOCK	POLLY
RUSSIAN	BUTTERFLY	FREE SPACE	LOUISE	FREELAND
DIONNE	GUYMON	CRANBERRY	NOBLE	ELZIRE
POND	JIM	HARDLY	LUCAS	POWER

Out Of The Dust

VERA	ROMNEY	DIONNE	POND	CEREUS
LIVIE	NYE	CRANBERRY	POWER	ELLIE
FLOR	POPPIES	FREE SPACE	FREELAND	RUSSIAN
CRADDOCK	RICE	ARLEY	KELBY	LUCAS
WHEAT	POLLY	ELZIRE	HARDLY	BAYARD

Out Of The Dust

LOUISE	JIM	FRANKLIN	NOBLE	GUYMON
REUBEN	BAYARD	HARDLY	ELZIRE	POLLY
WHEAT	LUCAS	FREE SPACE	ARLEY	RICE
CRADDOCK	RUSSIAN	FREELAND	BUTTERFLY	POPPIES
FLOR	ELLIE	POWER	CRANBERRY	NYE

Out Of The Dust

NOBLE	RUSSIAN	ARLEY	HARDLY	CEREUS
ROMNEY	LIVIE	BUTTERFLY	FREELAND	LOUISE
RICE	FLOR	FREE SPACE	POPPIES	DIONNE
CRADDOCK	REUBEN	NYE	POLLY	ELLIE
WHEAT	GUYMON	POND	VERA	FRANKLIN

Out Of The Dust

POWER	LUCAS	CRANBERRY	JIM	KELBY
ELZIRE	FRANKLIN	VERA	POND	GUYMON
WHEAT	ELLIE	FREE SPACE	NYE	REUBEN
CRADDOCK	DIONNE	POPPIES	BAYARD	FLOR
RICE	LOUISE	FREELAND	BUTTERFLY	LIVIE

Out Of The Dust

RICE	LOUISE	FLOR	ROMNEY	ARLEY
POND	ELLIE	KELBY	POLLY	POPPIES
LUCAS	VERA	FREE SPACE	REUBEN	CRANBERRY
CRADDOCK	DIONNE	WHEAT	GUYMON	POWER
LIVIE	BAYARD	NYE	NOBLE	JIM

Out Of The Dust

FREELAND	BUTTERFLY	RUSSIAN	ELZIRE	HARDLY
CEREUS	JIM	NOBLE	NYE	BAYARD
LIVIE	POWER	FREE SPACE	WHEAT	DIONNE
CRADDOCK	CRANBERRY	REUBEN	FRANKLIN	VERA
LUCAS	POPPIES	POLLY	KELBY	ELLIE

Out Of The Dust

JIM	NYE	REUBEN	BUTTERFLY	LUCAS
POWER	NOBLE	FRANKLIN	LOUISE	ARLEY
POLLY	GUYMON	FREE SPACE	CRADDOCK	WHEAT
HARDLY	RUSSIAN	VERA	ROMNEY	LIVIE
KELBY	RICE	FREELAND	CRANBERRY	CEREUS

Out Of The Dust

BAYARD	DIONNE	POPPIES	FLOR	ELLIE
POND	CEREUS	CRANBERRY	FREELAND	RICE
KELBY	LIVIE	FREE SPACE	VERA	RUSSIAN
HARDLY	WHEAT	CRADDOCK	ELZIRE	GUYMON
POLLY	ARLEY	LOUISE	FRANKLIN	NOBLE

Out Of The Dust

NOBLE	KELBY	POWER	FRANKLIN	WHEAT
POND	JIM	VERA	ELLIE	FREELAND
BAYARD	REUBEN	FREE SPACE	POPPIES	LUCAS
POLLY	LOUISE	NYE	ELZIRE	HARDLY
CEREUS	RICE	BUTTERFLY	CRADDOCK	LIVIE

Out Of The Dust

CRANBERRY	RUSSIAN	FLOR	ARLEY	DIONNE
ROMNEY	LIVIE	CRADDOCK	BUTTERFLY	RICE
CEREUS	HARDLY	FREE SPACE	NYE	LOUISE
POLLY	LUCAS	POPPIES	GUYMON	REUBEN
BAYARD	FREELAND	ELLIE	VERA	JIM

Out Of The Dust

CRADDOCK	CRANBERRY	RICE	JIM	LIVIE
HARDLY	LOUISE	DIONNE	POWER	ELLIE
FREELAND	POLLY	FREE SPACE	POPPIES	ELZIRE
WHEAT	RUSSIAN	FLOR	NYE	POND
BAYARD	GUYMON	VERA	REUBEN	NOBLE

Out Of The Dust

LUCAS	KELBY	ROMNEY	CEREUS	ARLEY
BUTTERFLY	NOBLE	REUBEN	VERA	GUYMON
BAYARD	POND	FREE SPACE	FLOR	RUSSIAN
WHEAT	ELZIRE	POPPIES	FRANKLIN	POLLY
FREELAND	ELLIE	POWER	DIONNE	LOUISE

Out Of The Dust

JIM	FLOR	RUSSIAN	LUCAS	FRANKLIN
WHEAT	REUBEN	CRANBERRY	NOBLE	HARDLY
ROMNEY	POWER	FREE SPACE	LOUISE	ARLEY
GUYMON	VERA	POPPIES	KELBY	FREELAND
CRADDOCK	POND	BAYARD	ELZIRE	RICE

Out Of The Dust

BUTTERFLY	CEREUS	POLLY	LIVIE	DIONNE
ELLIE	RICE	ELZIRE	BAYARD	POND
CRADDOCK	FREELAND	FREE SPACE	POPPIES	VERA
GUYMON	ARLEY	LOUISE	NYE	POWER
ROMNEY	HARDLY	NOBLE	CRANBERRY	REUBEN

Out Of The Dust

FRANKLIN	POPPIES	CRANBERRY	CEREUS	WHEAT
LOUISE	HARDLY	FLOR	KELBY	RUSSIAN
DIONNE	REUBEN	FREE SPACE	JIM	POLLY
ELZIRE	ROMNEY	POND	LIVIE	POWER
NOBLE	BUTTERFLY	BAYARD	CRADDOCK	FREELAND

Out Of The Dust

NYE	RICE	GUYMON	ELLIE	LUCAS
ARLEY	FREELAND	CRADDOCK	BAYARD	BUTTERFLY
NOBLE	POWER	FREE SPACE	POND	ROMNEY
ELZIRE	POLLY	JIM	VERA	REUBEN
DIONNE	RUSSIAN	KELBY	FLOR	HARDLY

Out Of The Dust

CRADDOCK	POPPIES	LOUISE	HARDLY	FLOR
BUTTERFLY	REUBEN	POND	POWER	RICE
FREELAND	ROMNEY	FREE SPACE	WHEAT	FRANKLIN
KELBY	ELLIE	ARLEY	DIONNE	LIVIE
BAYARD	GUYMON	VERA	LUCAS	JIM

Out Of The Dust

ELZIRE	RUSSIAN	NOBLE	CRANBERRY	CEREUS
NYE	JIM	LUCAS	VERA	GUYMON
BAYARD	LIVIE	FREE SPACE	ARLEY	ELLIE
KELBY	FRANKLIN	WHEAT	POLLY	ROMNEY
FREELAND	RICE	POWER	POND	REUBEN

Out Of The Dust

CEREUS	ELLIE	POND	LOUISE	KELBY
ROMNEY	BAYARD	RICE	DIONNE	REUBEN
NYE	POWER	FREE SPACE	FLOR	POLLY
JIM	FREELAND	ELZIRE	BUTTERFLY	POPPIES
ARLEY	NOBLE	RUSSIAN	LUCAS	GUYMON

Out Of The Dust

CRADDOCK	WHEAT	CRANBERRY	VERA	LIVIE
HARDLY	GUYMON	LUCAS	RUSSIAN	NOBLE
ARLEY	POPPIES	FREE SPACE	ELZIRE	FREELAND
JIM	POLLY	FLOR	FRANKLIN	POWER
NYE	REUBEN	DIONNE	RICE	BAYARD

Out Of The Dust

NOBLE	ELLIE	KELBY	ARLEY	FREELAND
LIVIE	POND	GUYMON	ROMNEY	JIM
CRADDOCK	FLOR	FREE SPACE	WHEAT	LUCAS
DIONNE	REUBEN	FRANKLIN	BAYARD	RUSSIAN
CRANBERRY	HARDLY	BUTTERFLY	POWER	NYE

Out Of The Dust

POLLY	ELZIRE	VERA	LOUISE	CEREUS
RICE	NYE	POWER	BUTTERFLY	HARDLY
CRANBERRY	RUSSIAN	FREE SPACE	FRANKLIN	REUBEN
DIONNE	LUCAS	WHEAT	POPPIES	FLOR
CRADDOCK	JIM	ROMNEY	GUYMON	POND

Out Of The Dust

RICE	ELLIE	NOBLE	BUTTERFLY	LIVIE
KELBY	JIM	POPPIES	BAYARD	CRADDOCK
WHEAT	POND	FREE SPACE	FRANKLIN	POLLY
ELZIRE	HARDLY	REUBEN	ARLEY	CEREUS
RUSSIAN	CRANBERRY	FLOR	GUYMON	LUCAS

Out Of The Dust

POWER	NYE	FREELAND	DIONNE	VERA
ROMNEY	LUCAS	GUYMON	FLOR	CRANBERRY
RUSSIAN	CEREUS	FREE SPACE	REUBEN	HARDLY
ELZIRE	POLLY	FRANKLIN	LOUISE	POND
WHEAT	CRADDOCK	BAYARD	POPPIES	JIM

Out Of The Dust Vocabulary Word List

No.	Word	Clue/Definition
1.	ANTISEPTIC	Destroyer of disease-carrying microorganisms
2.	BAWLING	Crying out loud
3.	BETROTHAL	Engagement
4.	BOXCAR	Fully enclosed railroad car used to carry freight
5.	BRITTLE	Fragile; likely to break
6.	CCC	Civilian Conservation Corps
7.	CHAFED	Worn sore by rubbing
8.	COMBINES	Harvesting machines
9.	COURT	Seek affection with the intent to romance; date
10.	CROUCHED	Stooped
11.	DAZZLED	Amazed or bewildered with spectacular display
12.	DEFORMED	Disfigured
13.	DESPERATE	Despairing; abandoning all hope
14.	DISTRACTED	Sidetracked; diverted
15.	DIVINING	Guessing
16.	DROUGHT	A long period of low rainfall
17.	DUNES	Hills or ridges of wind-blown sand (or dust)
18.	DUSTBOWL	Region reduced to aridity by drought and dust storms
19.	EXPOSING	Revealing
20.	FESTERED	Irritated; generating pus
21.	FLINCH	Recoil, as from something unpleasant
22.	GLAZING	Putting a thin, glassy coating on
23.	GLOWERING	Looking or staring angrily or sullenly
24.	GOPHERS	Burrowing rodents
25.	GRIME	Black dirt or soot clinging to a surface
26.	HARVEST	Gathering in of a crop
27.	HOARDING	Storing for future use
28.	HUNCHED	Bent
29.	IGNITE	Catch fire
30.	INTENTIONS	Plans; goals
31.	JEALOUS	Envious
32.	KEROSENE	A thin oil used as fuel
33.	KNOLL	Small, rounded hill
34.	LINDBERGHS	Charles and Ann, whose baby was stolen
35.	LONGING	Yearning or desire
36.	MASH	Mixture from which alcohol can be distilled
37.	MIGRANTS	Workers who travel around seeking work
38.	MOLDY	Musty or stale in odor or taste
39.	MOONSHINE	Illegally distilled whiskey
40.	MOTTLED	Marked by spots or blotches
41.	MUCK	Moist, sticky mixture, especially of mud and filth
42.	PANDOWDY	Dish baked with sugar with thick top crust
43.	PANHANDLE	Narrow strip of land projecting from a larger area
44.	PARCHED	Extremely dry; exposed to heat
45.	PRAIRIE	Large area of flat or rolling grassland
46.	PROSPECTS	Chances; possibilities
47.	QUINTUPLET	One of five offspring born in a single birth
48.	REVENGE	Punishment in return for insult or injury
49.	REVUE	A musical show
50.	SASSY	Impudent; brashly bold
51.	SCOWL	Frown

Out Of The Dust Vocabulary Word List Continued

No.	Word	Clue/Definition
52.	SEARING	Scorching or burning the surface of
53.	SHALE	Rock made of layers of sediment
54.	SIDING	Short section of railroad track
55.	SKETCH	Hasty or undetailed drawing or painting
56.	SNATCHED	Seized or grabbed
57.	SOD	Grass-covered surface soil held together by roots
58.	SOOTHE	Calm; quiet; ease or relieve
59.	SQUINTED	Looked at with eyes partly closed
60.	STUBBLE	Short, stiff stalks that remain after harvesting
61.	STUPOR	A state of reduced sensibility; a daze
62.	TART	Sour
63.	TESTY	Irritable; touchy
64.	THISTLE	Weedy plants with prickly leaves and purple flowers
65.	THROB	Pulsate; beat rapidly or violently
66.	TUFTS	Short cluster of strands, as of hair or grass
67.	TUMBLEWEED	Broken off plant that rolls around in the wind
68.	WARPED	Bent; twisted
69.	WHEEZY	Making a hoarse whistling sound
70.	WHIRLING	Rotating rapidly; spinning
71.	WHIRRED	Produced an airy, vibrating sound
72.	WHITTLED	Reduced gradually
73.	WINCE	Shrink back or start involuntarily, as in pain or distress
74.	WITHERED	Dried up; shriveled

Out Of The Dust Vocabulary Fill In The Blanks 1

_____ 1. Illegally distilled whiskey

_____ 2. Grass-covered surface soil held together by roots

_____ 3. Engagement

_____ 4. A state of reduced sensibility; a daze

_____ 5. Despairing; abandoning all hope

_____ 6. Dried up; shriveled

_____ 7. A musical show

_____ 8. Hills or ridges of wind-blown sand (or dust)

_____ 9. Marked by spots or blotches

_____ 10. Revealing

_____ 11. Making a hoarse whistling sound

_____ 12. Yearning or desire

_____ 13. Produced an airy, vibrating sound

_____ 14. Guessing

_____ 15. Rock made of layers of sediment

_____ 16. Irritable; touchy

_____ 17. Mixture from which alcohol can be distilled

_____ 18. Short section of railroad track

_____ 19. Sour

_____ 20. Pulsate; beat rapidly or violently

Out Of The Dust Vocabulary Fill In The Blanks 1 Answer Key

MOONSHINE	1. Illegally distilled whiskey
SOD	2. Grass-covered surface soil held together by roots
BETROTHAL	3. Engagement
STUPOR	4. A state of reduced sensibility; a daze
DESPERATE	5. Despairing; abandoning all hope
WITHERED	6. Dried up; shriveled
REVUE	7. A musical show
DUNES	8. Hills or ridges of wind-blown sand (or dust)
MOTTLED	9. Marked by spots or blotches
EXPOSING	10. Revealing
WHEEZY	11. Making a hoarse whistling sound
LONGING	12. Yearning or desire
WHIRRED	13. Produced an airy, vibrating sound
DIVINING	14. Guessing
SHALE	15. Rock made of layers of sediment
TESTY	16. Irritable; touchy
MASH	17. Mixture from which alcohol can be distilled
SIDING	18. Short section of railroad track
TART	19. Sour
THROB	20. Pulsate; beat rapidly or violently

Out Of The Dust Vocabulary Fill In The Blanks 2

_____ 1. Sour

_____ 2. Irritable; touchy

_____ 3. Dish baked with sugar with thick top crust

_____ 4. One of five offspring born in a single birth

_____ 5. Marked by spots or blotches

_____ 6. Produced an airy, vibrating sound

_____ 7. A musical show

_____ 8. Short cluster of strands, as of hair or grass

_____ 9. Narrow strip of land projecting from a larger area

_____ 10. Recoil, as from something unpleasant

_____ 11. Destroyer of disease-carrying microorganisms

_____ 12. Catch fire

_____ 13. Charles and Ann, whose baby was stolen

_____ 14. Making a hoarse whistling sound

_____ 15. Large area of flat or rolling grassland

_____ 16. Looking or staring angrily or sullenly

_____ 17. Workers who travel around seeking work

_____ 18. Burrowing rodents

_____ 19. Reduced gradually

_____ 20. Rotating rapidly; spinning

Out Of The Dust Vocabulary Fill In The Blanks 2 Answer Key

TART	1. Sour
TESTY	2. Irritable; touchy
PANDOWDY	3. Dish baked with sugar with thick top crust
QUINTUPLET	4. One of five offspring born in a single birth
MOTTLED	5. Marked by spots or blotches
WHIRRED	6. Produced an airy, vibrating sound
REVUE	7. A musical show
TUFTS	8. Short cluster of strands, as of hair or grass
PANHANDLE	9. Narrow strip of land projecting from a larger area
FLINCH	10. Recoil, as from something unpleasant
ANTISEPTIC	11. Destroyer of disease-carrying microorganisms
IGNITE	12. Catch fire
LINDBERGHS	13. Charles and Ann, whose baby was stolen
WHEEZY	14. Making a hoarse whistling sound
PRAIRIE	15. Large area of flat or rolling grassland
GLOWERING	16. Looking or staring angrily or sullenly
MIGRANTS	17. Workers who travel around seeking work
GOPHERS	18. Burrowing rodents
WHITTLED	19. Reduced gradually
WHIRLING	20. Rotating rapidly; spinning

Out Of The Dust Vocabulary Fill In The Blanks 3

_____   1. Crying out loud

_____   2. A long period of low rainfall

_____   3. Storing for future use

_____   4. Punishment in return for insult or injury

_____   5. Worn sore by rubbing

_____   6. Making a hoarse whistling sound

_____   7. Black dirt or soot clinging to a surface

_____   8. Civilian Conservation Corps

_____   9. Seek affection with the intent to romance; date

_____   10. Region reduced to aridity by drought and dust storms

_____   11. Chances; possibilities

_____   12. A state of reduced sensibility; a daze

_____   13. Calm; quiet; ease or relieve

_____   14. Musty or stale in odor or taste

_____   15. Engagement

_____   16. Workers who travel around seeking work

_____   17. A musical show

_____   18. Shrink back or start involuntarily, as in pain or distress

_____   19. Marked by spots or blotches

_____   20. Guessing

Out Of The Dust Vocabulary Fill In The Blanks 3 Answer Key

BAWLING	1. Crying out loud
DROUGHT	2. A long period of low rainfall
HOARDING	3. Storing for future use
REVENGE	4. Punishment in return for insult or injury
CHAFED	5. Worn sore by rubbing
WHEEZY	6. Making a hoarse whistling sound
GRIME	7. Black dirt or soot clinging to a surface
CCC	8. Civilian Conservation Corps
COURT	9. Seek affection with the intent to romance; date
DUSTBOWL	10. Region reduced to aridity by drought and dust storms
PROSPECTS	11. Chances; possibilities
STUPOR	12. A state of reduced sensibility; a daze
SOOTHE	13. Calm; quiet; ease or relieve
MOLDY	14. Musty or stale in odor or taste
BETROTHAL	15. Engagement
MIGRANTS	16. Workers who travel around seeking work
REVUE	17. A musical show
WINCE	18. Shrink back or start involuntarily, as in pain or distress
MOTTLED	19. Marked by spots or blotches
DIVINING	20. Guessing

Out Of The Dust Vocabulary Fill In The Blanks 4

_____ 1. Dried up; shriveled

_____ 2. Stooped

_____ 3. One of five offspring born in a single birth

_____ 4. Civilian Conservation Corps

_____ 5. Black dirt or soot clinging to a surface

_____ 6. A thin oil used as fuel

_____ 7. Small, rounded hill

_____ 8. Plans; goals

_____ 9. Illegally distilled whiskey

_____ 10. A state of reduced sensibility; a daze

_____ 11. Short, stiff stalks that remain after harvesting

_____ 12. Calm; quiet; ease or relieve

_____ 13. Large area of flat or rolling grassland

_____ 14. Irritated; generating pus

_____ 15. Short section of railroad track

_____ 16. Broken off plant that rolls around in the wind

_____ 17. Seized or grabbed

_____ 18. Burrowing rodents

_____ 19. Making a hoarse whistling sound

_____ 20. Harvesting machines

Out Of The Dust Vocabulary Fill In The Blanks 4 Answer Key

WITHERED	1. Dried up; shriveled
CROUCHED	2. Stooped
QUINTUPLET	3. One of five offspring born in a single birth
CCC	4. Civilian Conservation Corps
GRIME	5. Black dirt or soot clinging to a surface
KEROSENE	6. A thin oil used as fuel
KNOLL	7. Small, rounded hill
INTENTIONS	8. Plans; goals
MOONSHINE	9. Illegally distilled whiskey
STUPOR	10. A state of reduced sensibility; a daze
STUBBLE	11. Short, stiff stalks that remain after harvesting
SOOTHE	12. Calm; quiet; ease or relieve
PRAIRIE	13. Large area of flat or rolling grassland
FESTERED	14. Irritated; generating pus
SIDING	15. Short section of railroad track
TUMBLEWEED	16. Broken off plant that rolls around in the wind
SNATCHED	17. Seized or grabbed
GOPHERS	18. Burrowing rodents
WHEEZY	19. Making a hoarse whistling sound
COMBINES	20. Harvesting machines

Out Of The Dust Vocabulary Matching 1

___ 1. SOD — A. Mixture from which alcohol can be distilled
___ 2. INTENTIONS — B. Seek affection with the intent to romance; date
___ 3. SNATCHED — C. Fragile; likely to break
___ 4. SCOWL — D. Recoil, as from something unpleasant
___ 5. SOOTHE — E. Catch fire
___ 6. COURT — F. Envious
___ 7. IGNITE — G. Bent
___ 8. PRAIRIE — H. Frown
___ 9. SKETCH — I. Yearning or desire
___ 10. SHALE — J. Rock made of layers of sediment
___ 11. HUNCHED — K. Disfigured
___ 12. BRITTLE — L. Calm; quiet; ease or relieve
___ 13. MOTTLED — M. Hasty or undetailed drawing or painting
___ 14. GLAZING — N. Plans; goals
___ 15. JEALOUS — O. A thin oil used as fuel
___ 16. DEFORMED — P. Seized or grabbed
___ 17. REVENGE — Q. Stooped
___ 18. MASH — R. Punishment in return for insult or injury
___ 19. EXPOSING — S. Worn sore by rubbing
___ 20. LONGING — T. Revealing
___ 21. FLINCH — U. Black dirt or soot clinging to a surface
___ 22. CROUCHED — V. Large area of flat or rolling grassland
___ 23. GRIME — W. Grass-covered surface soil held together by roots
___ 24. KEROSENE — X. Putting a thin, glassy coating on
___ 25. CHAFED — Y. Marked by spots or blotches

Out Of The Dust Vocabulary Matching 1 Answer Key

W - 1. SOD
N - 2. INTENTIONS
P - 3. SNATCHED
H - 4. SCOWL
L - 5. SOOTHE
B - 6. COURT
E - 7. IGNITE
V - 8. PRAIRIE
M - 9. SKETCH
J - 10. SHALE
G - 11. HUNCHED
C - 12. BRITTLE
Y - 13. MOTTLED
X - 14. GLAZING
F - 15. JEALOUS
K - 16. DEFORMED
R - 17. REVENGE
A - 18. MASH
T - 19. EXPOSING
I - 20. LONGING
D - 21. FLINCH
Q - 22. CROUCHED
U - 23. GRIME
O - 24. KEROSENE
S - 25. CHAFED

A. Mixture from which alcohol can be distilled
B. Seek affection with the intent to romance; date
C. Fragile; likely to break
D. Recoil, as from something unpleasant
E. Catch fire
F. Envious
G. Bent
H. Frown
I. Yearning or desire
J. Rock made of layers of sediment
K. Disfigured
L. Calm; quiet; ease or relieve
M. Hasty or undetailed drawing or painting
N. Plans; goals
O. A thin oil used as fuel
P. Seized or grabbed
Q. Stooped
R. Punishment in return for insult or injury
S. Worn sore by rubbing
T. Revealing
U. Black dirt or soot clinging to a surface
V. Large area of flat or rolling grassland
W. Grass-covered surface soil held together by roots
X. Putting a thin, glassy coating on
Y. Marked by spots or blotches

Out Of The Dust Vocabulary Matching 2

____ 1. TART   A. Reduced gradually
____ 2. GLAZING   B. Hills or ridges of wind-blown sand (or dust)
____ 3. GLOWERING   C. Putting a thin, glassy coating on
____ 4. MOONSHINE   D. Sour
____ 5. COMBINES   E. Revealing
____ 6. PROSPECTS   F. Civilian Conservation Corps
____ 7. INTENTIONS   G. A thin oil used as fuel
____ 8. WHITTLED   H. Hasty or undetailed drawing or painting
____ 9. MIGRANTS   I. Small, rounded hill
____10. REVUE   J. Weedy plants with prickly leaves and purple flowers
____11. DISTRACTED   K. Sidetracked; diverted
____12. THISTLE   L. A musical show
____13. MUCK   M. Looking or staring angrily or sullenly
____14. WHIRRED   N. Workers who travel around seeking work
____15. CCC   O. Chances; possibilities
____16. MASH   P. Mixture from which alcohol can be distilled
____17. BETROTHAL   Q. Plans; goals
____18. KNOLL   R. Illegally distilled whiskey
____19. SHALE   S. Produced an airy, vibrating sound
____20. COURT   T. Crying out loud
____21. EXPOSING   U. Seek affection with the intent to romance; date
____22. DUNES   V. Moist, sticky mixture, especialy of mud and filth
____23. KEROSENE   W. Rock made of layers of sediment
____24. SKETCH   X. Harvesting machines
____25. BAWLING   Y. Engagement

Out Of The Dust Vocabulary Matching 2 Answer Key

D - 1. TART	A.	Reduced gradually
C - 2. GLAZING	B.	Hills or ridges of wind-blown sand (or dust)
M - 3. GLOWERING	C.	Putting a thin, glassy coating on
R - 4. MOONSHINE	D.	Sour
X - 5. COMBINES	E.	Revealing
O - 6. PROSPECTS	F.	Civilian Conservation Corps
Q - 7. INTENTIONS	G.	A thin oil used as fuel
A - 8. WHITTLED	H.	Hasty or undetailed drawing or painting
N - 9. MIGRANTS	I.	Small, rounded hill
L - 10. REVUE	J.	Weedy plants with prickly leaves and purple flowers
K - 11. DISTRACTED	K.	Sidetracked; diverted
J - 12. THISTLE	L.	A musical show
V - 13. MUCK	M.	Looking or staring angrily or sullenly
S - 14. WHIRRED	N.	Workers who travel around seeking work
F - 15. CCC	O.	Chances; possibilities
P - 16. MASH	P.	Mixture from which alcohol can be distilled
Y - 17. BETROTHAL	Q.	Plans; goals
I - 18. KNOLL	R.	Illegally distilled whiskey
W - 19. SHALE	S.	Produced an airy, vibrating sound
U - 20. COURT	T.	Crying out loud
E - 21. EXPOSING	U.	Seek affection with the intent to romance; date
B - 22. DUNES	V.	Moist, sticky mixture, especially of mud and filth
G - 23. KEROSENE	W.	Rock made of layers of sediment
H - 24. SKETCH	X.	Harvesting machines
T - 25. BAWLING	Y.	Engagement

Out Of The Dust Vocabulary Matching 3

___ 1. CCC A. Recoil, as from something unpleasant
___ 2. GRIME B. Black dirt or soot clinging to a surface
___ 3. JEALOUS C. Envious
___ 4. EXPOSING D. Irritable; touchy
___ 5. SCOWL E. Grass-covered surface soil held together by roots
___ 6. SOOTHE F. Scorching or burning the surface of
___ 7. SHALE G. Gathering in of a crop
___ 8. DIVINING H. Worn sore by rubbing
___ 9. BOXCAR I. Civilian Conservation Corps
___ 10. TART J. Reduced gradually
___ 11. LINDBERGHS K. Stooped
___ 12. BAWLING L. Shrink back or start involuntarily, as in pain or distress
___ 13. FLINCH M. Guessing
___ 14. CHAFED N. Looking or staring angrily or sullenly
___ 15. SEARING O. Illegally distilled whiskey
___ 16. HARVEST P. Hasty or undetailed drawing or painting
___ 17. MOONSHINE Q. Sidetracked; diverted
___ 18. TESTY R. Fully enclosed railroad car used to carry freight
___ 19. WHITTLED S. Revealing
___ 20. CROUCHED T. Crying out loud
___ 21. SOD U. Charles and Ann, whose baby was stolen
___ 22. SKETCH V. Rock made of layers of sediment
___ 23. WINCE W. Calm; quiet; ease or relieve
___ 24. DISTRACTED X. Frown
___ 25. GLOWERING Y. Sour

Out Of The Dust Vocabulary Matching 3 Answer Key

I - 1.	CCC	A. Recoil, as from something unpleasant
B - 2.	GRIME	B. Black dirt or soot clinging to a surface
C - 3.	JEALOUS	C. Envious
S - 4.	EXPOSING	D. Irritable; touchy
X - 5.	SCOWL	E. Grass-covered surface soil held together by roots
W - 6.	SOOTHE	F. Scorching or burning the surface of
V - 7.	SHALE	G. Gathering in of a crop
M - 8.	DIVINING	H. Worn sore by rubbing
R - 9.	BOXCAR	I. Civilian Conservation Corps
Y - 10.	TART	J. Reduced gradually
U - 11.	LINDBERGHS	K. Stooped
T - 12.	BAWLING	L. Shrink back or start involuntarily, as in pain or distress
A - 13.	FLINCH	M. Guessing
H - 14.	CHAFED	N. Looking or staring angrily or sullenly
F - 15.	SEARING	O. Illegally distilled whiskey
G - 16.	HARVEST	P. Hasty or undetailed drawing or painting
O - 17.	MOONSHINE	Q. Sidetracked; diverted
D - 18.	TESTY	R. Fully enclosed railroad car used to carry freight
J - 19.	WHITTLED	S. Revealing
K - 20.	CROUCHED	T. Crying out loud
E - 21.	SOD	U. Charles and Ann, whose baby was stolen
P - 22.	SKETCH	V. Rock made of layers of sediment
L - 23.	WINCE	W. Calm; quiet; ease or relieve
Q - 24.	DISTRACTED	X. Frown
N - 25.	GLOWERING	Y. Sour

Out Of The Dust Vocabulary Matching 4

___ 1. GLOWERING   A. Disfigured
___ 2. WHITTLED   B. A thin oil used as fuel
___ 3. KNOLL   C. Storing for future use
___ 4. DISTRACTED   D. Bent; twisted
___ 5. TUMBLEWEED   E. Scorching or burning the surface of
___ 6. SCOWL   F. A long period of low rainfall
___ 7. KEROSENE   G. Sidetracked; diverted
___ 8. STUPOR   H. Bent
___ 9. FESTERED   I. Short cluster of strands, as of hair or grass
___10. HUNCHED   J. Hasty or undetailed drawing or painting
___11. WARPED   K. Dried up; shriveled
___12. SASSY   L. Envious
___13. SKETCH   M. Looking or staring angrily or sullenly
___14. INTENTIONS   N. Crying out loud
___15. EXPOSING   O. Irritated; generating pus
___16. SEARING   P. Grass-covered surface soil held together by roots
___17. HOARDING   Q. Impudent; brashly bold
___18. TUFTS   R. Engagement
___19. BETROTHAL   S. Frown
___20. BAWLING   T. Revealing
___21. DROUGHT   U. Broken off plant that rolls around in the wind
___22. DEFORMED   V. Reduced gradually
___23. JEALOUS   W. Plans; goals
___24. SOD   X. Small, rounded hill
___25. WITHERED   Y. A state of reduced sensibility; a daze

Out Of The Dust Vocabulary Matching 4 Answer Key

M - 1.	GLOWERING	A.	Disfigured
V - 2.	WHITTLED	B.	A thin oil used as fuel
X - 3.	KNOLL	C.	Storing for future use
G - 4.	DISTRACTED	D.	Bent; twisted
U - 5.	TUMBLEWEED	E.	Scorching or burning the surface of
S - 6.	SCOWL	F.	A long period of low rainfall
B - 7.	KEROSENE	G.	Sidetracked; diverted
Y - 8.	STUPOR	H.	Bent
O - 9.	FESTERED	I.	Short cluster of strands, as of hair or grass
H - 10.	HUNCHED	J.	Hasty or undetailed drawing or painting
D - 11.	WARPED	K.	Dried up; shriveled
Q - 12.	SASSY	L.	Envious
J - 13.	SKETCH	M.	Looking or staring angrily or sullenly
W - 14.	INTENTIONS	N.	Crying out loud
T - 15.	EXPOSING	O.	Irritated; generating pus
E - 16.	SEARING	P.	Grass-covered surface soil held together by roots
C - 17.	HOARDING	Q.	Impudent; brashly bold
I - 18.	TUFTS	R.	Engagement
R - 19.	BETROTHAL	S.	Frown
N - 20.	BAWLING	T.	Revealing
F - 21.	DROUGHT	U.	Broken off plant that rolls around in the wind
A - 22.	DEFORMED	V.	Reduced gradually
L - 23.	JEALOUS	W.	Plans; goals
P - 24.	SOD	X.	Small, rounded hill
K - 25.	WITHERED	Y.	A state of reduced sensibility; a daze

Out Of The Dust Vocabulary Magic Squares 1

Match the definition with the vocabulary word. Put your answers in the magic squares below. When your answers are correct, all columns and rows will add to the same number.

A. BAWLING
B. GOPHERS
C. LONGING
D. GLAZING
E. WARPED
F. TESTY
G. PANHANDLE
H. REVENGE
I. WHIRLING
J. WHEEZY
K. TUFTS
L. HUNCHED
M. WITHERED
N. MIGRANTS
O. PRAIRIE
P. SASSY

1. Workers who travel around seeking work
2. Narrow strip of land projecting from a larger area
3. Bent
4. Crying out loud
5. Short cluster of strands, as of hair or grass
6. Burrowing rodents
7. Dried up; shriveled
8. Punishment in return for insult or injury
9. Bent; twisted
10. Impudent; brashly bold
11. Yearning or desire
12. Making a hoarse whistling sound
13. Putting a thin, glassy coating on
14. Rotating rapidly; spinning
15. Irritable; touchy
16. Large area of flat or rolling grassland

A=	B=	C=	D=
E=	F=	G=	H=
I=	J=	K=	L=
M=	N=	O=	P=

Out Of The Dust Vocabulary Magic Squares 1 Answer Key

Match the definition with the vocabulary word. Put your answers in the magic squares below. When your answers are correct, all columns and rows will add to the same number.

A. BAWLING
B. GOPHERS
C. LONGING
D. GLAZING
E. WARPED
F. TESTY
G. PANHANDLE
H. REVENGE
I. WHIRLING
J. WHEEZY
K. TUFTS
L. HUNCHED
M. WITHERED
N. MIGRANTS
O. PRAIRIE
P. SASSY

1. Workers who travel around seeking work
2. Narrow strip of land projecting from a larger area
3. Bent
4. Crying out loud
5. Short cluster of strands, as of hair or grass
6. Burrowing rodents
7. Dried up; shriveled
8. Punishment in return for insult or injury
9. Bent; twisted
10. Impudent; brashly bold
11. Yearning or desire
12. Making a hoarse whistling sound
13. Putting a thin, glassy coating on
14. Rotating rapidly; spinning
15. Irritable; touchy
16. Large area of flat or rolling grassland

A=4	B=6	C=11	D=13
E=9	F=15	G=2	H=8
I=14	J=12	K=5	L=3
M=7	N=1	O=16	P=10

Out Of The Dust Vocabulary Magic Squares 2

Match the definition with the vocabulary word. Put your answers in the magic squares below. When your answers are correct, all columns and rows will add to the same number.

A. GLAZING
B. MOLDY
C. CHAFED
D. PRAIRIE
E. DUNES
F. DEFORMED
G. SHALE
H. CROUCHED
I. SKETCH
J. LONGING
K. SCOWL
L. REVENGE
M. FLINCH
N. LINDBERGHS
O. INTENTIONS
P. MIGRANTS

1. Stooped
2. Putting a thin, glassy coating on
3. Musty or stale in odor or taste
4. Rock made of layers of sediment
5. Yearning or desire
6. Plans; goals
7. Workers who travel around seeking work
8. Hasty or undetailed drawing or painting
9. Frown
10. Charles and Ann, whose baby was stolen
11. Recoil, as from something unpleasant
12. Punishment in return for insult or injury
13. Hills or ridges of wind-blown sand (or dust)
14. Large area of flat or rolling grassland
15. Worn sore by rubbing
16. Disfigured

A=	B=	C=	D=
E=	F=	G=	H=
I=	J=	K=	L=
M=	N=	O=	P=

Out Of The Dust Vocabulary Magic Squares 2 Answer Key

Match the definition with the vocabulary word. Put your answers in the magic squares below. When your answers are correct, all columns and rows will add to the same number.

A. GLAZING
B. MOLDY
C. CHAFED
D. PRAIRIE
E. DUNES
F. DEFORMED
G. SHALE
H. CROUCHED
I. SKETCH
J. LONGING
K. SCOWL
L. REVENGE
M. FLINCH
N. LINDBERGHS
O. INTENTIONS
P. MIGRANTS

1. Stooped
2. Putting a thin, glassy coating on
3. Musty or stale in odor or taste
4. Rock made of layers of sediment
5. Yearning or desire
6. Plans; goals
7. Workers who travel around seeking work
8. Hasty or undetailed drawing or painting
9. Frown
10. Charles and Ann, whose baby was stolen
11. Recoil, as from something unpleasant
12. Punishment in return for insult or injury
13. Hills or ridges of wind-blown sand (or dust)
14. Large area of flat or rolling grassland
15. Worn sore by rubbing
16. Disfigured

A=2	B=3	C=15	D=14
E=13	F=16	G=4	H=1
I=8	J=5	K=9	L=12
M=11	N=10	O=6	P=7

Out Of The Dust Vocabulary Magic Squares 3

Match the definition with the vocabulary word. Put your answers in the magic squares below. When your answers are correct, all columns and rows will add to the same number.

A. THROB
B. SOOTHE
C. THISTLE
D. MOONSHINE
E. WHEEZY
F. SEARING
G. WINCE
H. CCC
I. HUNCHED
J. GRIME
K. PROSPECTS
L. BETROTHAL
M. PANDOWDY
N. TUFTS
O. SIDING
P. IGNITE

1. Scorching or burning the surface of
2. Bent
3. Short section of railroad track
4. Illegally distilled whiskey
5. Dish baked with sugar with thick top crust
6. Calm; quiet; ease or relieve
7. Civilian Conservation Corps
8. Chances; possibilities
9. Weedy plants with prickly leaves and purple flowers
10. Catch fire
11. Black dirt or soot clinging to a surface
12. Making a hoarse whistling sound
13. Engagement
14. Shrink back or start involuntarily, as in pain or distress
15. Pulsate; beat rapidly or violently
16. Short cluster of strands, as of hair or grass

A=	B=	C=	D=
E=	F=	G=	H=
I=	J=	K=	L=
M=	N=	O=	P=

Out Of The Dust Vocabulary Magic Squares 3 Answer Key

Match the definition with the vocabulary word. Put your answers in the magic squares below. When your answers are correct, all columns and rows will add to the same number.

A. THROB
B. SOOTHE
C. THISTLE
D. MOONSHINE
E. WHEEZY
F. SEARING
G. WINCE
H. CCC
I. HUNCHED
J. GRIME
K. PROSPECTS
L. BETROTHAL
M. PANDOWDY
N. TUFTS
O. SIDING
P. IGNITE

1. Scorching or burning the surface of
2. Bent
3. Short section of railroad track
4. Illegally distilled whiskey
5. Dish baked with sugar with thick top crust
6. Calm; quiet; ease or relieve
7. Civilian Conservation Corps
8. Chances; possibilities
9. Weedy plants with prickly leaves and purple flowers
10. Catch fire
11. Black dirt or soot clinging to a surface
12. Making a hoarse whistling sound
13. Engagement
14. Shrink back or start involuntarily, as in pain or distress
15. Pulsate; beat rapidly or violently
16. Short cluster of strands, as of hair or grass

A=15	B=6	C=9	D=4
E=12	F=1	G=14	H=7
I=2	J=11	K=8	L=13
M=5	N=16	O=3	P=10

Out Of The Dust Vocabulary Magic Squares 4

Match the definition with the vocabulary word. Put your answers in the magic squares below. When your answers are correct, all columns and rows will add to the same number.

A. WHIRRED
B. STUBBLE
C. TESTY
D. FESTERED
E. DISTRACTED
F. PRAIRIE
G. DAZZLED
H. BRITTLE
I. HUNCHED
J. SASSY
K. LINDBERGHS
L. EXPOSING
M. SCOWL
N. REVENGE
O. REVUE
P. WINCE

1. Frown
2. Large area of flat or rolling grassland
3. Fragile; likely to break
4. A musical show
5. Revealing
6. Irritable; touchy
7. Produced an airy, vibrating sound
8. Impudent; brashly bold
9. Charles and Ann, whose baby was stolen
10. Irritated; generating pus
11. Short, stiff stalks that remain after harvesting
12. Bent
13. Punishment in return for insult or injury
14. Sidetracked; diverted
15. Amazed or bewildered with spectacular display
16. Shrink back or start involuntarily, as in pain or distress

A=	B=	C=	D=
E=	F=	G=	H=
I=	J=	K=	L=
M=	N=	O=	P=

Out Of The Dust Vocabulary Magic Squares 4 Answer Key

Match the definition with the vocabulary word. Put your answers in the magic squares below. When your answers are correct, all columns and rows will add to the same number.

A. WHIRRED
B. STUBBLE
C. TESTY
D. FESTERED
E. DISTRACTED
F. PRAIRIE
G. DAZZLED
H. BRITTLE
I. HUNCHED
J. SASSY
K. LINDBERGHS
L. EXPOSING
M. SCOWL
N. REVENGE
O. REVUE
P. WINCE

1. Frown
2. Large area of flat or rolling grassland
3. Fragile; likely to break
4. A musical show
5. Revealing
6. Irritable; touchy
7. Produced an airy, vibrating sound
8. Impudent; brashly bold
9. Charles and Ann, whose baby was stolen
10. Irritated; generating pus
11. Short, stiff stalks that remain after harvesting
12. Bent
13. Punishment in return for insult or injury
14. Sidetracked; diverted
15. Amazed or bewildered with spectacular display
16. Shrink back or start involuntarily, as in pain or distress

A=7	B=11	C=6	D=10
E=14	F=2	G=15	H=3
I=12	J=8	K=9	L=5
M=1	N=13	O=4	P=16

Out Of The Dust Vocabulary Word Search 1

```
F P G T S E A R I N G N I N I V I D
L R L S H T B S E H T O C S V P M B
I A A I U I U X G C H N P R J S U T
N I Z D N F S B D E R R I H W Q C B
C R I I C T P T B T O O D V E V K E
H I N N H D E S L L B H U U T R L B
N E G G E H E N R E E S W C N A S N
Y D W O D N A P T S N A T C H E D W
B A W L I N G R Z I R M O S C E S G
W X W B W S A F V P O U D L T S D B
F I M R X T L J E E R N O A E A V M
G O N D S U H D D T S N S H K S T G
C R H C R P F D M A G T D T S S J R
T D I M E O E X S I Z E Y O M Y E C
E V Z M S R U F N C F Z L R Y V S Y
S C V T E V V G L A O F L T U L Y D
T Q F T D E R E H T I W H E E Z Y R
Y U S K Y C G C K T S N L B D D F Y
T E D B O X C A R R O R E V E N G E
F D I S T R A C T E D E H C R A P R
```

A long period of low rainfall (7)
A musical show (5)
A state of reduced sensibility; a daze (6)
Amazed or bewildered with spectacular display (7)
Bent (7)
Bent; twisted (6)
Black dirt or soot clinging to a surface (5)
Burrowing rodents (7)
Calm; quiet; ease or relieve (6)
Civilian Conservation Corps (3)
Crying out loud (7)
Dish baked with sugar with thick top crust (8)
Dried up; shriveled (8)
Engagement (9)
Extremely dry; exposed to heat (7)
Frown (5)
Fully enclosed railroad car used to carry freight (6)
Gathering in of a crop (7)
Grass-covered surface soil held together by roots (3)
Guessing (8)
Harvesting machines (8)
Hasty or undetailed drawing or painting (6)
Hills or ridges of wind-blown sand (or dust) (5)
Impudent; brashly bold (5)
Irritable; touchy (5)

Irritated; generating pus (8)
Large area of flat or rolling grassland (7)
Making a hoarse whistling sound (6)
Mixture from which alcohol can be distilled (4)
Moist, sticky mixture, especially of mud and filth (4)
Plans; goals (10)
Produced an airy, vibrating sound (7)
Pulsate; beat rapidly or violently (5)
Punishment in return for insult or injury (7)
Putting a thin, glassy coating on (7)
Recoil, as from something unpleasant (6)
Rock made of layers of sediment (5)
Scorching or burning the surface of (7)
Seek affection with the intent to romance; date (5)
Seized or grabbed (8)
Short cluster of strands, as of hair or grass (5)
Short section of railroad track (6)
Short, stiff stalks that remain after harvesting (7)
Shrink back or start involuntarily, as in pain or distress (5)
Sidetracked; diverted (10)
Sour (4)
Stooped (8)
Weedy plants with prickly leaves and purple flowers (7)
Worn sore by rubbing (6)
Yearning or desire (7)

Out Of The Dust Vocabulary Word Search 1 Answer Key

```
F P G T S E A R I N G N I N I V I D
L R L S H T E H T O O S   M
I A A I U I U   C H   P   U
N I Z D N   S B D E R R I H W   C
C R I I C T   T B   O O D   E   K E
H I N N H   E S L L B H U U   R   L
  E G G E   H E N   E E S W C N A S
Y D W O D N A P T S N A T C H E D
B A W L I N G R   I R M O S C E S
W   B   S A   V P O U   L T S D
  I M   T   E E R N O A E A
G O N D   U   D D T S N S H K S
C R   C R P   D   A G T D T S S   R
T   I   E O E   S I Z E   O   Y E
E   M S R U   N C F Z   R   V
S     T E   G   A O   L T U
T   F T D E R E H T I W H E E Z Y
Y U S     C   C   T S   L B D
T E   B O X C A R   O R E V E N G E
F D I S T R A C T E D E H C R A P
```

A long period of low rainfall (7)
A musical show (5)
A state of reduced sensibility; a daze (6)
Amazed or bewildered with spectacular display (7)
Bent (7)
Bent; twisted (6)
Black dirt or soot clinging to a surface (5)
Burrowing rodents (7)
Calm; quiet; ease or relieve (6)
Civilian Conservation Corps (3)
Crying out loud (7)
Dish baked with sugar with thick top crust (8)
Dried up; shriveled (8)
Engagement (9)
Extremely dry; exposed to heat (7)
Frown (5)
Fully enclosed railroad car used to carry freight (6)
Gathering in of a crop (7)
Grass-covered surface soil held together by roots (3)
Guessing (8)
Harvesting machines (8)
Hasty or undetailed drawing or painting (6)
Hills or ridges of wind-blown sand (or dust) (5)
Impudent; brashly bold (5)
Irritable; touchy (5)

Irritated; generating pus (8)
Large area of flat or rolling grassland (7)
Making a hoarse whistling sound (6)
Mixture from which alcohol can be distilled (4)
Moist, sticky mixture, especially of mud and filth (4)
Plans; goals (10)
Produced an airy, vibrating sound (7)
Pulsate; beat rapidly or violently (5)
Punishment in return for insult or injury (7)
Putting a thin, glassy coating on (7)
Recoil, as from something unpleasant (6)
Rock made of layers of sediment (5)
Scorching or burning the surface of (7)
Seek affection with the intent to romance; date (5)
Seized or grabbed (8)
Short cluster of strands, as of hair or grass (5)
Short section of railroad track (6)
Short, stiff stalks that remain after harvesting (7)
Shrink back or start involuntarily, as in pain or distress (5)
Sidetracked; diverted (10)
Sour (4)
Stooped (8)
Weedy plants with prickly leaves and purple flowers (7)
Worn sore by rubbing (6)
Yearning or desire (7)

Out Of The Dust Vocabulary Word Search 2

```
T U F T S M K P W M Q R E V E N G E
H A N D M E O T B H U G S L L O N K
R Z R S H B V L E N I C R Z J T I G
O C S T R W R H D S N R K I H Z N S
B T O N P K H I S Y T K L I M C I R
L O K P A V U I T W U Y S I N E V D
S T K G D T N N R T P T K A N T I G
P R O S P E C T S R L W O C S G D Z
M U G K V G H H C E E E Q E Q S Z J
L O D O E Q E A E R T D V R U D Y M
C C C S P R D R N D W R R D I R S B
R M X Y R H O L R T A G E U N O E Z
B O X C A R E S O H I D V N T U A Q
C T T M I Y J R E N S S U E E G R J
S T N A R G I M S N G I E S D H I T
H L R X I X N A K O E I D P G T N L
L E Q V E B R S E W D J N I T Q G W
K D F L I N C H T J V V G G N I T W
D U S T B O W L C I G N I T E G C Q
G L A Z I N G S H A L E C N I W R K
```

A long period of low rainfall (7)
A musical show (5)
A thin oil used as fuel (8)
Bent (7)
Black dirt or soot clinging to a surface (5)
Burrowing rodents (7)
Calm; quiet; ease or relieve (6)
Catch fire (6)
Chances; possibilities (9)
Civilian Conservation Corps (3)
Destroyer of disease-carrying microorganisms (10)
Fragile; likely to break (7)
Frown (5)
Fully enclosed railroad car used to carry freight (6)
Gathering in of a crop (7)
Grass-covered surface soil held together by roots (3)
Guessing (8)
Hasty or undetailed drawing or painting (6)
Hills or ridges of wind-blown sand (or dust) (5)
Impudent; brashly bold (5)
Irritable; touchy (5)
Large area of flat or rolling grassland (7)
Looked at with eyes partly closed (8)
Marked by spots or blotches (7)
Mixture from which alcohol can be distilled (4)
Moist, sticky mixture, especially of mud and filth (4)
Musty or stale in odor or taste (5)
One of five offspring born in a single birth (10)
Produced an airy, vibrating sound (7)
Pulsate; beat rapidly or violently (5)
Punishment in return for insult or injury (7)
Putting a thin, glassy coating on (7)
Recoil, as from something unpleasant (6)
Region reduced to aridity by drought and dust storms (8)
Rock made of layers of sediment (5)
Rotating rapidly; spinning (8)
Scorching or burning the surface of (7)
Seek affection with the intent to romance; date (5)
Seized or grabbed (8)
Short cluster of strands, as of hair or grass (5)
Short section of railroad track (6)
Shrink back or start involuntarily, as in pain or distress (5)
Small, rounded hill (5)
Sour (4)
Weedy plants with prickly leaves and purple flowers (7)
Workers who travel around seeking work (8)
Yearning or desire (7)

Out Of The Dust Vocabulary Word Search 2 Answer Key

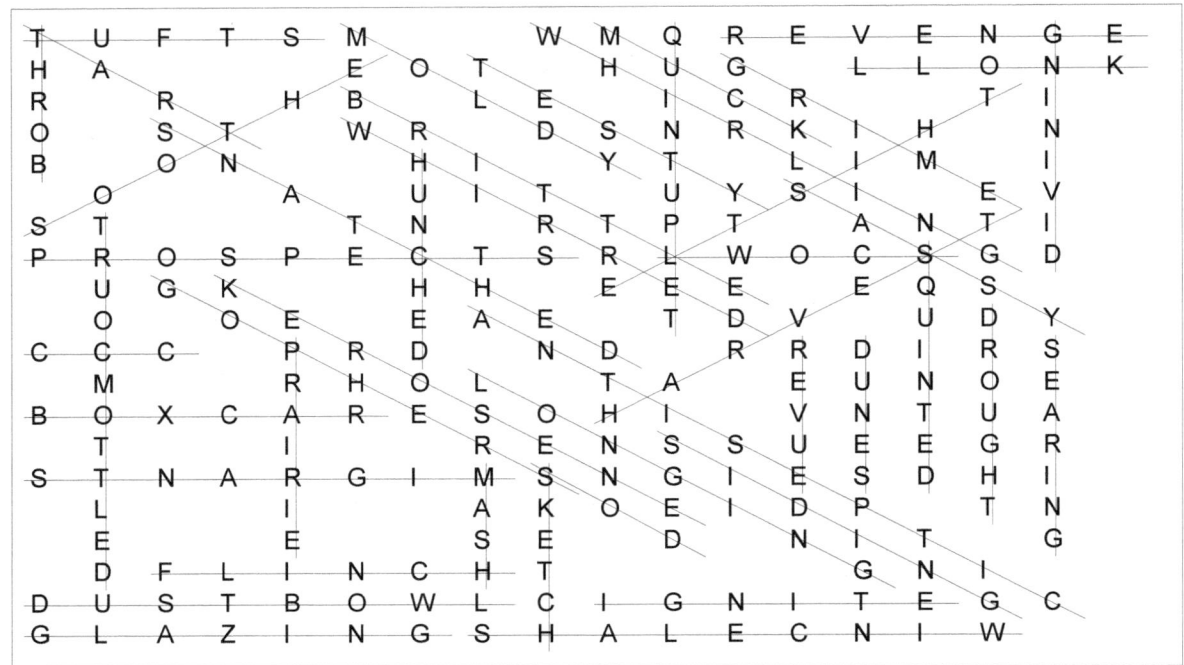

A long period of low rainfall (7)
A musical show (5)
A thin oil used as fuel (8)
Bent (7)
Black dirt or soot clinging to a surface (5)
Burrowing rodents (7)
Calm; quiet; ease or relieve (6)
Catch fire (6)
Chances; possibilities (9)
Civilian Conservation Corps (3)
Destroyer of disease-carrying microorganisms (10)
Fragile; likely to break (7)
Frown (5)
Fully enclosed railroad car used to carry freight (6)
Gathering in of a crop (7)
Grass-covered surface soil held together by roots (3)
Guessing (8)
Hasty or undetailed drawing or painting (6)
Hills or ridges of wind-blown sand (or dust) (5)
Impudent; brashly bold (5)
Irritable; touchy (5)
Large area of flat or rolling grassland (7)
Looked at with eyes partly closed (8)
Marked by spots or blotches (7)
Mixture from which alcohol can be distilled (4)
Moist, sticky mixture, especially of mud and filth (4)
Musty or stale in odor or taste (5)
One of five offspring born in a single birth (10)
Produced an airy, vibrating sound (7)
Pulsate; beat rapidly or violently (5)
Punishment in return for insult or injury (7)
Putting a thin, glassy coating on (7)
Recoil, as from something unpleasant (6)
Region reduced to aridity by drought and dust storms (8)
Rock made of layers of sediment (5)
Rotating rapidly; spinning (8)
Scorching or burning the surface of (7)
Seek affection with the intent to romance; date (5)
Seized or grabbed (8)
Short cluster of strands, as of hair or grass (5)
Short section of railroad track (6)
Shrink back or start involuntarily, as in pain or distress (5)
Small, rounded hill (5)
Sour (4)
Weedy plants with prickly leaves and purple flowers (7)
Workers who travel around seeking work (8)
Yearning or desire (7)

Out Of The Dust Vocabulary Word Search 3

```
N W J H B O X C A R J D T V C B S D S N
V N H J U P R A I R I E H T O O S E T M
W H A I J N S V O C C L A Q C R U P F Y
T B R Y R Y C P Y N Z T M L P H E R U R
D S V T S L U H I N N T U N O T N A T Z
E I E R P T I W E B Y I C G J U E W A L
T D S A S A U N I D A H K C C S S L N P
N Z T T R C R B G T Z W R L C T O H T W
I D S P R I Y C B D H T L L B N R L I M
U R C G E A N T H L C E I I G A E B S M
Q O O N U H C G E E E N R B N R K I E W
S U W I V C Z T L S D K D E T G D K P M
S G L D E T P D E B T Q W U D I Z N T S
W H I R R E D Y E D H Y D H N M D O I K
R T G A J K S R E E I O E G E E Y L C S
E G N O N S G L L F S V Y X S E S L G D
V O I H A H Z Z W A T S I P P D Z N F P
E P T S S Z S M P H L G E N G O I Y N Z
N H E G A S H T A C E R G V I Z S F W L
G E J D T W A F Z S A I P X A N M I X V
E R M O T T L E D T H M O L D Y G Q N Q
Y S F E S T E R E D K E G F L I N C H G
```

ANTISEPTIC	EXPOSING	KNOLL	SCOWL	THISTLE
BAWLING	FESTERED	LINDBERGHS	SEARING	THROB
BOXCAR	FLINCH	MASH	SHALE	TUFTS
CCC	GLAZING	MIGRANTS	SIDING	WARPED
CHAFED	GOPHERS	MOLDY	SKETCH	WHEEZY
COURT	GRIME	MOTTLED	SOD	WHIRLING
DAZZLED	HARVEST	MUCK	SOOTHE	WHIRRED
DESPERATE	HOARDING	PARCHED	SQUINTED	WHITTLED
DISTRACTED	HUNCHED	PRAIRIE	STUBBLE	WINCE
DIVINING	IGNITE	REVENGE	STUPOR	WITHERED
DROUGHT	JEALOUS	REVUE	TART	
DUNES	KEROSENE	SASSY	TESTY	

Out Of The Dust Vocabulary Word Search 3 Answer Key

ANTISEPTIC	EXPOSING	KNOLL	SCOWL	THISTLE
BAWLING	FESTERED	LINDBERGHS	SEARING	THROB
BOXCAR	FLINCH	MASH	SHALE	TUFTS
CCC	GLAZING	MIGRANTS	SIDING	WARPED
CHAFED	GOPHERS	MOLDY	SKETCH	WHEEZY
COURT	GRIME	MOTTLED	SOD	WHIRLING
DAZZLED	HARVEST	MUCK	SOOTHE	WHIRRED
DESPERATE	HOARDING	PARCHED	SQUINTED	WHITTLED
DISTRACTED	HUNCHED	PRAIRIE	STUBBLE	WINCE
DIVINING	IGNITE	REVENGE	STUPOR	WITHERED
DROUGHT	JEALOUS	REVUE	TART	
DUNES	KEROSENE	SASSY	TESTY	

Out Of The Dust Vocabulary Word Search 4

```
S L A H T O R T E B L O N G I N G P B Y
T E D E H C N U H R R I G N I T E O D V
U K A D L W Z M F D E I D X F W R Y E D
B W G R I M E B W L P V T N X H T H H V
B R H Z I G B L J B I R U T T B H B C Q
L W E I Y N V E H S C N A E L S I A U Y
E D H V R C G W P L H R C I G E S W O N
R R G A E R W E S T A A N H R T T L R E
P O B M R N E E X K F T L Y C I L I C D
M U C K J V G D E R E T S E F S E N U D
X G Y Z M J E E S N D T S P T Y T I G S D
F H Q Y T M F S T W R S C X C W U Y O G
N T Q R R Y H I T S O Y P H H P V F O Y
H L U O G L O W E R I N G A B T E S T Y
J O F P V N A N P J W D J G N O M C H S
C E Q M S H R G V R W T I E O D X C E W
D S A S S Y D E L D N A H N A P O C J P
T T O A D Z I M V A L R R V G L H W A Y
V U M D M E N M O L Z T J P S Q O E D R
S P Y R H E G R O L B I S S E T J U R Y
M O O N S H I N E F D K N C B D D R S S
N R Z P G W K Q L N G Y V G S C O W L C
```

BAWLING	FESTERED	JEALOUS	REVENGE	STUPOR
BETROTHAL	FLINCH	KNOLL	REVUE	TART
BOXCAR	GLAZING	LONGING	SASSY	TESTY
BRITTLE	GLOWERING	MASH	SCOWL	THISTLE
CCC	GOPHERS	MOLDY	SEARING	THROB
CHAFED	GRIME	MOONSHINE	SHALE	TUFTS
COURT	HARVEST	MUCK	SIDING	TUMBLEWEED
CROUCHED	HOARDING	PANDOWDY	SKETCH	WARPED
DEFORMED	HUNCHED	PANHANDLE	SOD	WHEEZY
DROUGHT	IGNITE	PRAIRIE	SOOTHE	WHIRRED
DUNES	INTENTIONS	PROSPECTS	STUBBLE	WINCE

Out Of The Dust Vocabulary Word Search 4 Answer Key

```
S L A H T O R T E B L O N G I N G       B
T E D E H C N U H R R I G N I T E   O   D E
U   A       M F E I           R     H
B W G R I M E B   L P V T       H   B E
B R H I     L   I R U T T   T H   B C
L E I N     E   S N A E L       I   A U
E D H V R G W   H A C I   E     S W   O E
  R A E R E E     K T L     C   T L   R
M U C K V G D E R E T S E F   S E N   C D
  G   A R N E E   N D T P     T I G   U
  H   T M E E   T     S C     W U     S
  T R R H     I     S O     P H         O
    U O G L O W E R I N G A B T E S T Y
    O F   N A   P       D J G N O   C H S
  C E   S H R G       W T I E O D X C   E
  D S A S S Y D E L D N A H N A P O C   E
    T O A   Z I M   A L R R   G L H W A
    U M D   E N   O L Z T     P   O E D R
    P     E G   O L   I         E   U R Y
    M O O N S H I N E   D     D   R S S
          R           W K                   G S C O W L
```

BAWLING   FESTERED   JEALOUS   REVENGE   STUPOR

BETROTHAL   FLINCH   KNOLL   REVUE   TART

BOXCAR   GLAZING   LONGING   SASSY   TESTY

BRITTLE   GLOWERING   MASH   SCOWL   THISTLE

CCC   GOPHERS   MOLDY   SEARING   THROB

CHAFED   GRIME   MOONSHINE   SHALE   TUFTS

COURT   HARVEST   MUCK   SIDING   TUMBLEWEED

CROUCHED   HOARDING   PANDOWDY   SKETCH   WARPED

DEFORMED   HUNCHED   PANHANDLE   SOD   WHEEZY

DROUGHT   IGNITE   PRAIRIE   SOOTHE   WHIRRED

DUNES   INTENTIONS   PROSPECTS   STUBBLE   WINCE

Out Of The Dust Vocabulary Crossword 1

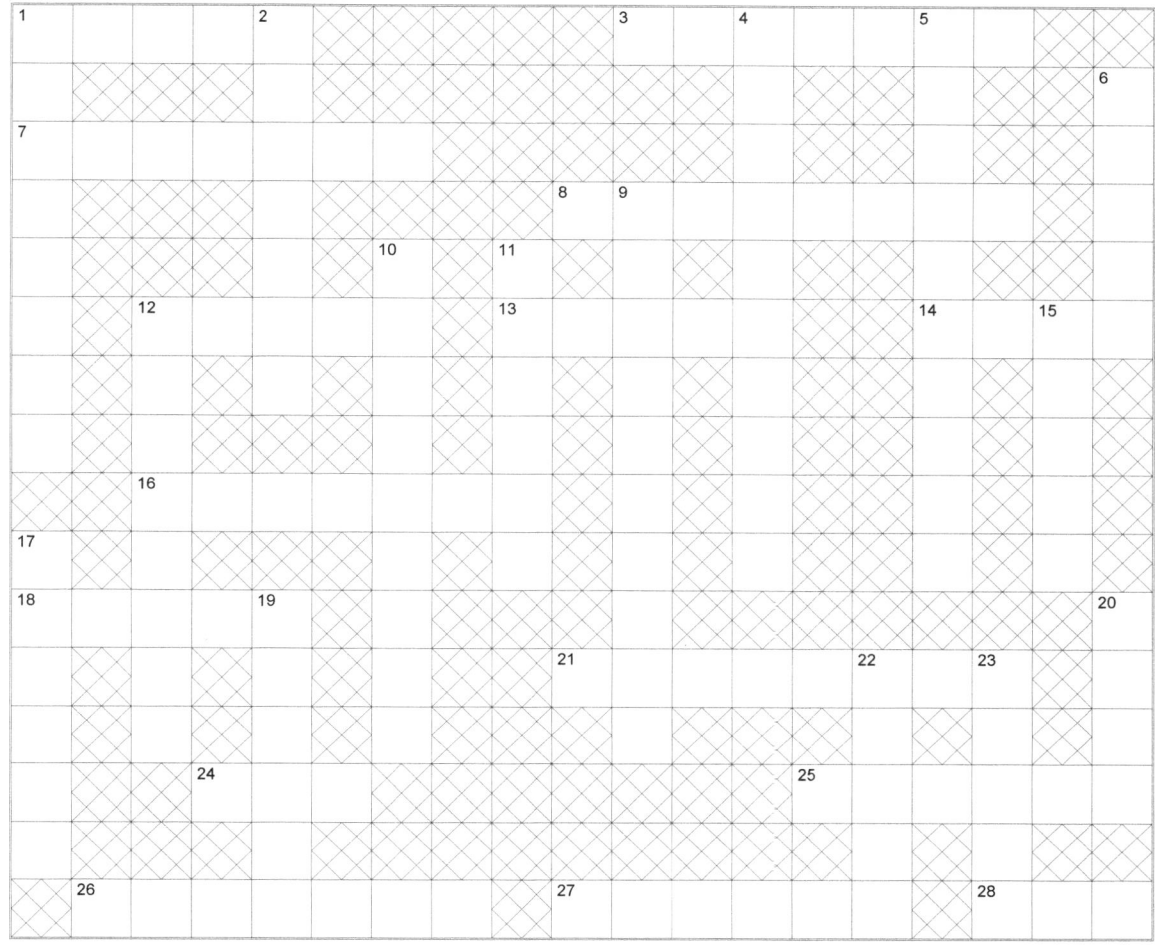

Across
1. Small, rounded hill
3. Large area of flat or rolling grassland
7. Punishment in return for insult or injury
8. Looked at with eyes partly closed
12. Shrink back or start involuntarily, as in pain or distress
13. Black dirt or soot clinging to a surface
14. Sour
16. Gathering in of a crop
18. Pulsate; beat rapidly or violently
21. Disfigured
24. Civilian Conservation Corps
25. Recoil, as from something unpleasant
26. Scorching or burning the surface of
27. Making a hoarse whistling sound
28. Grass-covered surface soil held together by roots

Down
1. A thin oil used as fuel
2. Yearning or desire
4. Destroyer of disease-carrying microorganisms
5. Plans; goals
6. Seek affection with the intent to romance; date
9. One of five offspring born in a single birth
10. Despairing; abandoning all hope
11. Catch fire
12. Dried up; shriveled
15. A musical show
17. A state of reduced sensibility; a daze
19. Fully enclosed railroad car used to carry freight
20. Mixture from which alcohol can be distilled
22. Musty or stale in odor or taste
23. Hills or ridges of wind-blown sand (or dust)

Out Of The Dust Vocabulary Crossword 1 Answer Key

Across
1. Small, rounded hill
3. Large area of flat or rolling grassland
7. Punishment in return for insult or injury
8. Looked at with eyes partly closed
12. Shrink back or start involuntarily, as in pain or distress
13. Black dirt or soot clinging to a surface
14. Sour
16. Gathering in of a crop
18. Pulsate; beat rapidly or violently
21. Disfigured
24. Civilian Conservation Corps
25. Recoil, as from something unpleasant
26. Scorching or burning the surface of
27. Making a hoarse whistling sound
28. Grass-covered surface soil held together by roots

Down
1. A thin oil used as fuel
2. Yearning or desire
4. Destroyer of disease-carrying microorganisms
5. Plans; goals
6. Seek affection with the intent to romance; date
9. One of five offspring born in a single birth
10. Despairing; abandoning all hope
11. Catch fire
12. Dried up; shriveled
15. A musical show
17. A state of reduced sensibility; a daze
19. Fully enclosed railroad car used to carry freight
20. Mixture from which alcohol can be distilled
22. Musty or stale in odor or taste
23. Hills or ridges of wind-blown sand (or dust)

Out Of The Dust Vocabulary Crossword 2

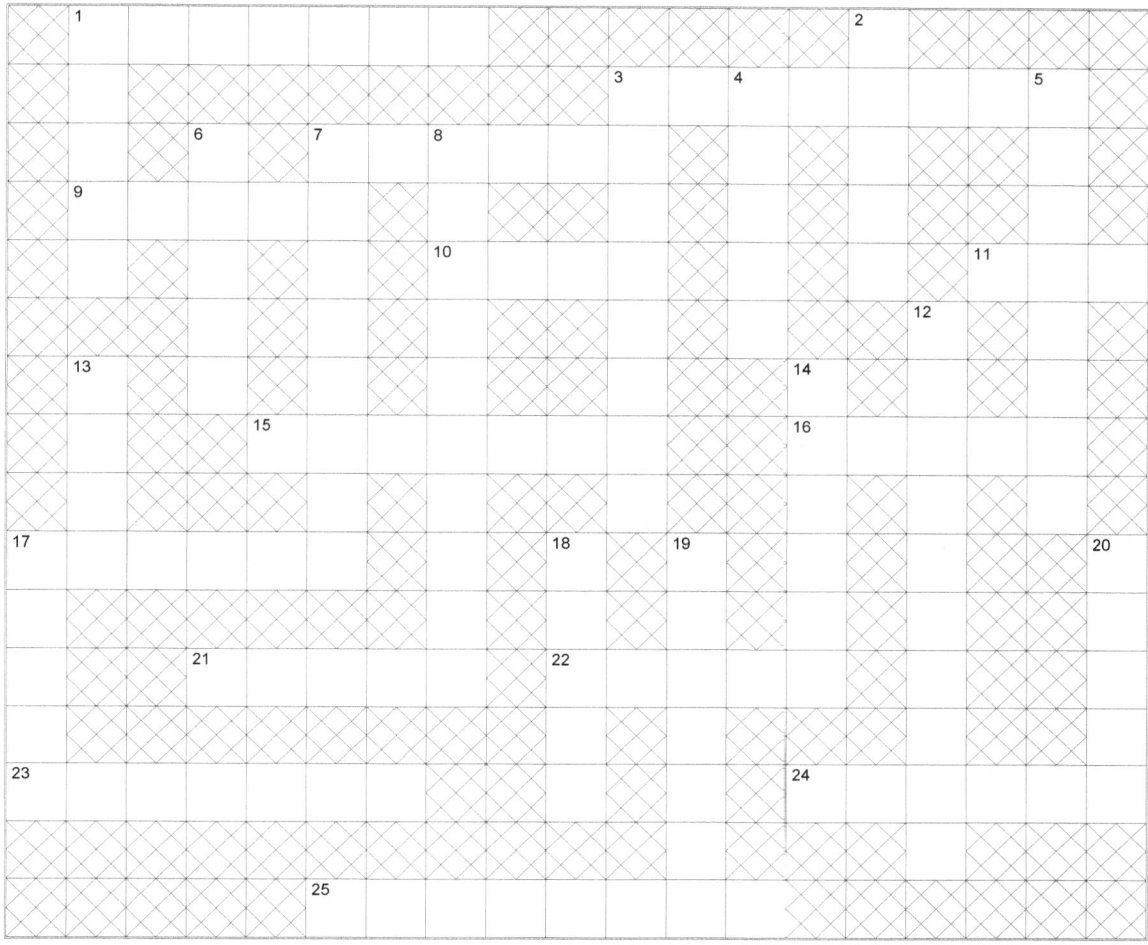

Across
1. Scorching or burning the surface of
3. Dried up; shriveled
7. Recoil, as from something unpleasant
9. Shrink back or start involuntarily, as in pain or distress
10. Sour
11. Grass-covered surface soil held together by roots
15. Fragile; likely to break
16. Black dirt or soot clinging to a surface
17. Worn sore by rubbing
21. Hills or ridges of wind-blown sand (or dust)
22. Rock made of layers of sediment
23. Weedy plants with prickly leaves and purple flowers
24. Making a hoarse whistling sound
25. Harvesting machines

Down
1. Frown
2. A musical show
3. Reduced gradually
4. Pulsate; beat rapidly or violently
5. Disfigured
6. Small, rounded hill
7. Irritated; generating pus
8. Plans; goals
12. One of five offspring born in a single birth
13. Mixture from which alcohol can be distilled
14. Catch fire
17. Seek affection with the intent to romance; date
18. Impudent; brashly bold
19. Large area of flat or rolling grassland
20. Musty or stale in odor or taste

Out Of The Dust Vocabulary Crossword 2 Answer Key

Across
1. Scorching or burning the surface of
3. Dried up; shriveled
7. Recoil, as from something unpleasant
9. Shrink back or start involuntarily, as in pain or distress
10. Sour
11. Grass-covered surface soil held together by roots
15. Fragile; likely to break
16. Black dirt or soot clinging to a surface
17. Worn sore by rubbing
21. Hills or ridges of wind-blown sand (or dust)
22. Rock made of layers of sediment
23. Weedy plants with prickly leaves and purple flowers
24. Making a hoarse whistling sound
25. Harvesting machines

Down
1. Frown
2. A musical show
3. Reduced gradually
4. Pulsate; beat rapidly or violently
5. Disfigured
6. Small, rounded hill
7. Irritated; generating pus
8. Plans; goals
12. One of five offspring born in a single birth
13. Mixture from which alcohol can be distilled
14. Catch fire
17. Seek affection with the intent to romance; date
18. Impudent; brashly bold
19. Large area of flat or rolling grassland
20. Musty or stale in odor or taste

Out Of The Dust Vocabulary Crossword 3

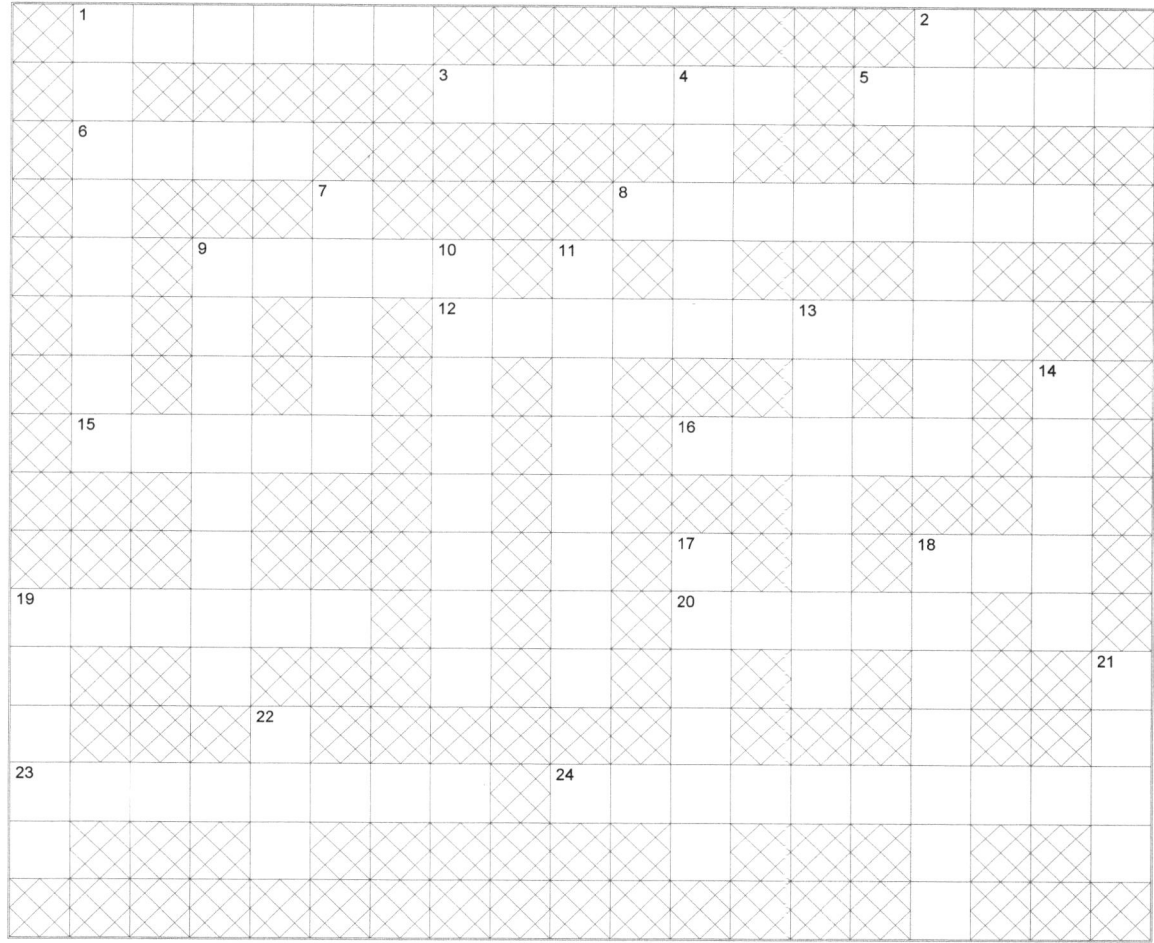

Across
1. Worn sore by rubbing
3. Recoil, as from something unpleasant
5. A musical show
6. Moist, sticky mixture, especially of mud and filth
8. Region reduced to aridity by drought and dust storms
9. Hills or ridges of wind-blown sand (or dust)
12. One of five offspring born in a single birth
15. Frown
16. Rock made of layers of sediment
18. Grass-covered surface soil held together by roots
19. Making a hoarse whistling sound
20. Black dirt or soot clinging to a surface
23. Stooped
24. Plans; goals

Down
1. Harvesting machines
2. A thin oil used as fuel
4. Seek affection with the intent to romance; date
7. Small, rounded hill
9. Disfigured
10. Looked at with eyes partly closed
11. Dried up; shriveled
13. Large area of flat or rolling grassland
14. Musty or stale in odor or taste
17. Catch fire
18. Scorching or burning the surface of
19. Shrink back or start involuntarily, as in pain or distress
21. Mixture from which alcohol can be distilled
22. Civilian Conservation Corps

Out Of The Dust Vocabulary Crossword 3 Answer Key

Across
1. Worn sore by rubbing
3. Recoil, as from something unpleasant
5. A musical show
6. Moist, sticky mixture, especially of mud and filth
8. Region reduced to aridity by drought and dust storms
9. Hills or ridges of wind-blown sand (or dust)
12. One of five offspring born in a single birth
15. Frown
16. Rock made of layers of sediment
18. Grass-covered surface soil held together by roots
19. Making a hoarse whistling sound
20. Black dirt or soot clinging to a surface
23. Stooped
24. Plans; goals

Down
1. Harvesting machines
2. A thin oil used as fuel
4. Seek affection with the intent to romance; date
7. Small, rounded hill
9. Disfigured
10. Looked at with eyes partly closed
11. Dried up; shriveled
13. Large area of flat or rolling grassland
14. Musty or stale in odor or taste
17. Catch fire
18. Scorching or burning the surface of
19. Shrink back or start involuntarily, as in pain or distress
21. Mixture from which alcohol can be distilled
22. Civilian Conservation Corps

Out Of The Dust Vocabulary Crossword 4

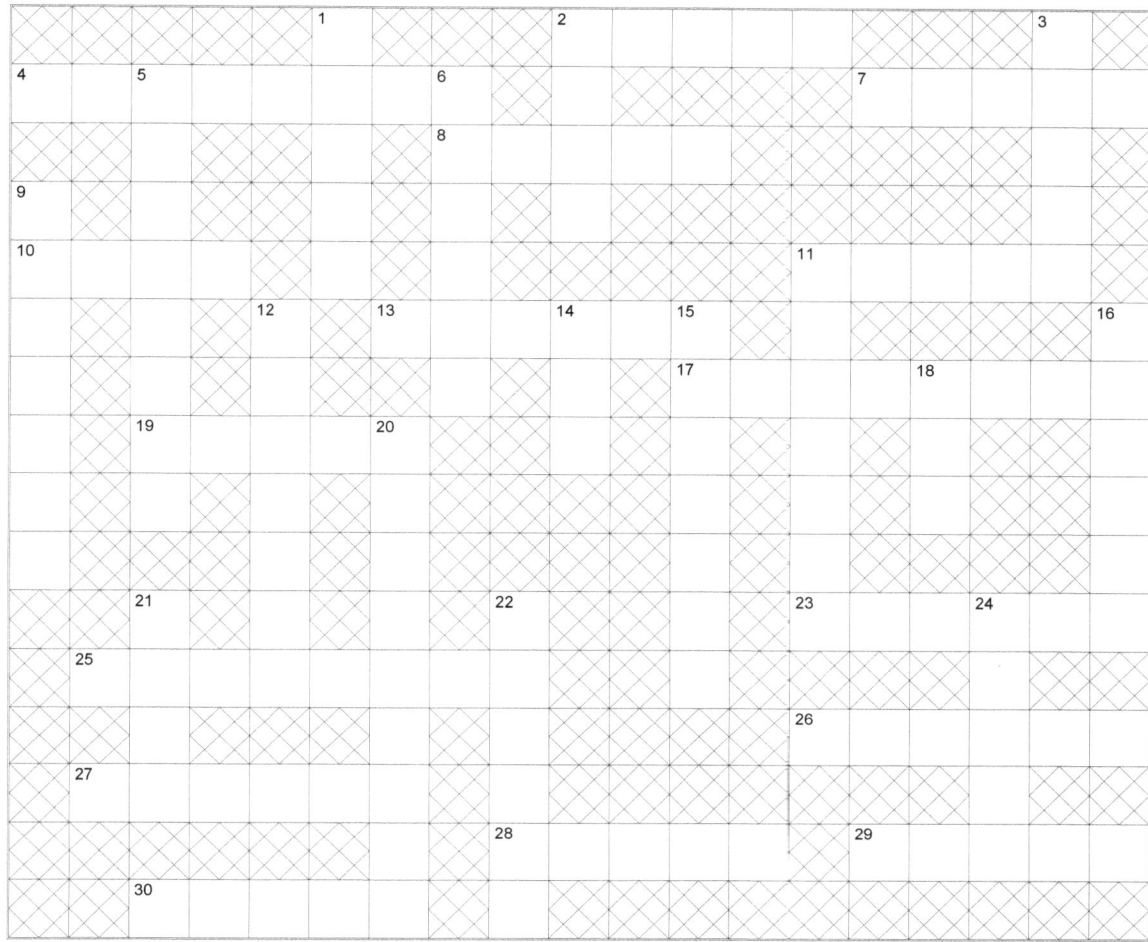

Across
2. Musty or stale in odor or taste
4. Harvesting machines
7. Hills or ridges of wind-blown sand (or dust)
8. Irritable; touchy
10. Sour
11. Black dirt or soot clinging to a surface
13. Fully enclosed railroad car used to carry freight
17. Revealing
19. Pulsate; beat rapidly or violently
23. Calm; quiet; ease or relieve
25. Region reduced to aridity by drought and dust storms
26. Worn sore by rubbing
27. Hasty or undetailed drawing or painting
28. Seek affection with the intent to romance; date
29. Impudent; brashly bold
30. Frown

Down
1. Small, rounded hill
2. Mixture from which alcohol can be distilled
3. A musical show
5. Workers who travel around seeking work
6. A state of reduced sensibility; a daze
9. Short, stiff stalks that remain after harvesting
11. Burrowing rodents
12. Gathering in of a crop
14. Civilian Conservation Corps
15. Punishment in return for insult or injury
16. Catch fire
18. Grass-covered surface soil held together by roots
20. Engagement
21. Moist, sticky mixture, especially of mud and filth
22. Recoil, as from something unpleasant
24. Short cluster of strands, as of hair or grass

Out Of The Dust Vocabulary Crossword 4 Answer Key

					¹K			²M	O	L	D	Y			³R	
⁴C	O	⁵M	B	I	N	E	⁶S		A			⁷D	U	N	E	S
		I			O		⁸T	E	S	T	Y				V	
⁹S		G			L		U		H						U	
¹⁰T	A	R	T		L		P				¹¹G	R	I	M	E	
U		A	¹²H	¹³B	O	X	¹⁴C	A	¹⁵R		O				¹⁶I
B		N	A				C		¹⁷E	X	P	¹⁸S	I	N	G
B	¹⁹T	H	R	O	²⁰B		C		V		H		O		N
L	S		V		E				E		E		D		I
E			E		T				N		R				T
	²¹M		S		R		²²F		G		²³S	O	O	²⁴T	H	E
²⁵D	U	S	T	B	O	W	L		E					U	
	C				T		I				²⁶C	H	A	F	E	D
²⁷S	K	E	T	C	H		N							T	
					²⁸A		C	O	U	R	T		²⁹S	A	S	S	Y
	³⁰S	C	O	W	L		H								

Across
2. Musty or stale in odor or taste
4. Harvesting machines
7. Hills or ridges of wind-blown sand (or dust)
8. Irritable; touchy
10. Sour
11. Black dirt or soot clinging to a surface
13. Fully enclosed railroad car used to carry freight
17. Revealing
19. Pulsate; beat rapidly or violently
23. Calm; quiet; ease or relieve
25. Region reduced to aridity by drought and dust storms
26. Worn sore by rubbing
27. Hasty or undetailed drawing or painting
28. Seek affection with the intent to romance; date
29. Impudent; brashly bold
30. Frown

Down
1. Small, rounded hill
2. Mixture from which alcohol can be distilled
3. A musical show
5. Workers who travel around seeking work
6. A state of reduced sensibility; a daze
9. Short, stiff stalks that remain after harvesting
11. Burrowing rodents
12. Gathering in of a crop
14. Civilian Conservation Corps
15. Punishment in return for insult or injury
16. Catch fire
18. Grass-covered surface soil held together by roots
20. Engagement
21. Moist, sticky mixture, especially of mud and filth
22. Recoil, as from something unpleasant
24. Short cluster of strands, as of hair or grass

Out Of The Dust Vocabulary Juggle Letters 1

1. DTELHIWT = 1. _____
   Reduced gradually

2. DINNIIVG = 2. _____
   Guessing

3. NITESITNON = 3. _____
   Plans; goals

4. ALBIWGN = 4. _____
   Crying out loud

5. VRETASH = 5. _____
   Gathering in of a crop

6. OGNGILN = 6. _____
   Yearning or desire

7. LIHFCN = 7. _____
   Recoil, as from something unpleasant

8. SAMH = 8. _____
   Mixture from which alcohol can be distilled

9. TGUOHRD = 9. _____
   A long period of low rainfall

10. OEDFDMER = 10. _____
    Disfigured

11. HPCDAER = 11. _____
    Extremely dry; exposed to heat

12. IGIDNS = 12. _____
    Short section of railroad track

13. GSERPHO = 13. _____
    Burrowing rodents

14. UMKC = 14. _____
    Moist, sticky mixture, especially of mud and filth

15. LTERIBT = 15. _____
    Fragile; likely to break

Out Of The Dust Vocabulary Juggle Letters 1 Answer Key

1. DTELHIWT = 1. WHITTLED
Reduced gradually

2. DINNIIVG = 2. DIVINING
Guessing

3. NITESITNON = 3. INTENTIONS
Plans; goals

4. ALBIWGN = 4. BAWLING
Crying out loud

5. VRETASH = 5. HARVEST
Gathering in of a crop

6. OGNGILN = 6. LONGING
Yearning or desire

7. LIHFCN = 7. FLINCH
Recoil, as from something unpleasant

8. SAMH = 8. MASH
Mixture from which alcohol can be distilled

9. TGUOHRD = 9. DROUGHT
A long period of low rainfall

10. OEDFDMER = 10. DEFORMED
Disfigured

11. HPCDAER = 11. PARCHED
Extremely dry; exposed to heat

12. IGIDNS = 12. SIDING
Short section of railroad track

13. GSERPHO = 13. GOPHERS
Burrowing rodents

14. UMKC = 14. MUCK
Moist, sticky mixture, especially of mud and filth

15. LTERIBT = 15. BRITTLE
Fragile; likely to break

Out Of The Dust Vocabulary Juggle Letters 2

1. CRAPDEH = 1. _____
   Extremely dry; exposed to heat

2. NMRATSGI = 2. _____
   Workers who travel around seeking work

3. IPEACTNTIS = 3. _____
   Destroyer of disease-carrying microorganisms

4. TUSTF = 4. _____
   Short cluster of strands, as of hair or grass

5. SIRBGNDELH = 5. _____
   Charles and Ann, whose baby was stolen

6. TDIWTLEH = 6. _____
   Reduced gradually

7. NIIGET = 7. _____
   Catch fire

8. OESNIGXP = 8. _____
   Revealing

9. TOEABRTHL = 9. _____
   Engagement

10. UQUELTINTP =10. _____
    One of five offspring born in a single birth

11. TOGURDH =11. _____
    A long period of low rainfall

12. IECWN =12. _____
    Shrink back or start involuntarily, as in pain or distress

13. TIHESLT =13. _____
    Weedy plants with prickly leaves and purple flowers

14. EEWDTIRH =14. _____
    Dried up; shriveled

15. HSMA =15. _____
    Mixture from which alcohol can be distilled

Out Of The Dust Vocabulary Juggle Letters 2 Answer Key

1. CRAPDEH = 1. PARCHED
   Extremely dry; exposed to heat

2. NMRATSGI = 2. MIGRANTS
   Workers who travel around seeking work

3. IPEACTNTIS = 3. ANTISEPTIC
   Destroyer of disease-carrying microorganisms

4. TUSTF = 4. TUFTS
   Short cluster of strands, as of hair or grass

5. SIRBGNDELH = 5. LINDBERGHS
   Charles and Ann, whose baby was stolen

6. TDIWTLEH = 6. WHITTLED
   Reduced gradually

7. NIIGET = 7. IGNITE
   Catch fire

8. OESNIGXP = 8. EXPOSING
   Revealing

9. TOEABRTHL = 9. BETROTHAL
   Engagement

10. UQUELTINTP = 10. QUINTUPLET
    One of five offspring born in a single birth

11. TOGURDH = 11. DROUGHT
    A long period of low rainfall

12. IECWN = 12. WINCE
    Shrink back or start involuntarily, as in pain or distress

13. TIHESLT = 13. THISTLE
    Weedy plants with prickly leaves and purple flowers

14. EEWDTIRH = 14. WITHERED
    Dried up; shriveled

15. HSMA = 15. MASH
    Mixture from which alcohol can be distilled

Out Of The Dust Vocabulary Juggle Letters 3

1. RPEOSHG = 1. _____
   Burrowing rodents

2. SYSSA = 2. _____
   Impudent; brashly bold

3. CWSLO = 3. _____
   Frown

4. HDANCETS = 4. _____
   Seized or grabbed

5. ANGILGZ = 5. _____
   Putting a thin, glassy coating on

6. SECBOMNI = 6. _____
   Harvesting machines

7. NNOLIGG = 7. _____
   Yearning or desire

8. FUSTT = 8. _____
   Short cluster of strands, as of hair or grass

9. CRAOXB = 9. _____
   Fully enclosed railroad car used to carry freight

10. SOD = 10. _____
    Grass-covered surface soil held together by roots

11. MSAH = 11. _____
    Mixture from which alcohol can be distilled

12. EERUV = 12. _____
    A musical show

13. ASNIGER = 13. _____
    Scorching or burning the surface of

14. NLKOL = 14. _____
    Small, rounded hill

15. EOKRSEEN = 15. _____
    A thin oil used as fuel

Out Of The Dust Vocabulary Juggle Letters 3 Answer Key

1. RPEOSHG = 1. GOPHERS
Burrowing rodents

2. SYSSA = 2. SASSY
Impudent; brashly bold

3. CWSLO = 3. SCOWL
Frown

4. HDANCETS = 4. SNATCHED
Seized or grabbed

5. ANGILGZ = 5. GLAZING
Putting a thin, glassy coating on

6. SECBOMNI = 6. COMBINES
Harvesting machines

7. NNOLIGG = 7. LONGING
Yearning or desire

8. FUSTT = 8. TUFTS
Short cluster of strands, as of hair or grass

9. CRAOXB = 9. BOXCAR
Fully enclosed railroad car used to carry freight

10. SOD = 10. SOD
Grass-covered surface soil held together by roots

11. MSAH = 11. MASH
Mixture from which alcohol can be distilled

12. EERUV = 12. REVUE
A musical show

13. ASNIGER = 13. SEARING
Scorching or burning the surface of

14. NLKOL = 14. KNOLL
Small, rounded hill

15. EOKRSEEN = 15. KEROSENE
A thin oil used as fuel

Out Of The Dust Vocabulary Juggle Letters 4

1. NOESEKRE = 1. _____
   A thin oil used as fuel

2. ISDDTREATC = 2. _____
   Sidetracked; diverted

3. RIRAEPI = 3. _____
   Large area of flat or rolling grassland

4. TSEYT = 4. _____
   Irritable; touchy

5. IOLGGWRNE = 5. _____
   Looking or staring angrily or sullenly

6. DHCAEPR = 6. _____
   Extremely dry; exposed to heat

7. AESTERPED = 7. _____
   Despairing; abandoning all hope

8. TPENATICIS = 8. _____
   Destroyer of disease-carrying microorganisms

9. XEPNSOGI = 9. _____
   Revealing

10. DSO = 10. _____
    Grass-covered surface soil held together by roots

11. IVDGININ = 11. _____
    Guessing

12. XOACBR = 12. _____
    Fully enclosed railroad car used to carry freight

13. RWHDETIE = 13. _____
    Dried up; shriveled

14. HZEYWE = 14. _____
    Making a hoarse whistling sound

15. EGVNREE = 15. _____
    Punishment in return for insult or injury

Out Of The Dust Vocabulary Juggle Letters 4 Answer Key

1. NOESEKRE = 1. KEROSENE
   A thin oil used as fuel

2. ISDDTREATC = 2. DISTRACTED
   Sidetracked; diverted

3. RIRAEPI = 3. PRAIRIE
   Large area of flat or rolling grassland

4. TSEYT = 4. TESTY
   Irritable; touchy

5. IOLGGWRNE = 5. GLOWERING
   Looking or staring angrily or sullenly

6. DHCAEPR = 6. PARCHED
   Extremely dry; exposed to heat

7. AESTERPED = 7. DESPERATE
   Despairing; abandoning all hope

8. TPENATICIS = 8. ANTISEPTIC
   Destroyer of disease-carrying microorganisms

9. XEPNSOGI = 9. EXPOSING
   Revealing

10. DSO = 10. SOD
    Grass-covered surface soil held together by roots

11. IVDGININ = 11. DIVINING
    Guessing

12. XOACBR = 12. BOXCAR
    Fully enclosed railroad car used to carry freight

13. RWHDETIE = 13. WITHERED
    Dried up; shriveled

14. HZEYWE = 14. WHEEZY
    Making a hoarse whistling sound

15. EGVNREE = 15. REVENGE
    Punishment in return for insult or injury

ANTISEPTIC	Destroyer of disease-carrying microorganisms
BAWLING	Crying out loud
BETROTHAL	Engagement
BOXCAR	Fully enclosed railroad car used to carry freight
BRITTLE	Fragile; likely to break
CCC	Civilian Conservation Corps

CHAFED	Worn sore by rubbing
COMBINES	Harvesting machines
COURT	Seek affection with the intent to romance; date
CROUCHED	Stooped
DAZZLED	Amazed or bewildered with spectacular display
DEFORMED	Disfigured

DESPERATE	Despairing; abandoning all hope
DISTRACTED	Sidetracked; diverted
DIVINING	Guessing
DROUGHT	A long period of low rainfall
DUNES	Hills or ridges of wind-blown sand (or dust)
DUSTBOWL	Region reduced to aridity by drought and dust storms

EXPOSING	Revealing
FESTERED	Irritated; generating pus
FLINCH	Recoil, as from something unpleasant
GLAZING	Putting a thin, glassy coating on
GLOWERING	Looking or staring angrily or sullenly
GOPHERS	Burrowing rodents

GRIME	Black dirt or soot clinging to a surface
HARVEST	Gathering in of a crop
HOARDING	Storing for future use
HUNCHED	Bent
IGNITE	Catch fire
INTENTIONS	Plans; goals

JEALOUS	Envious
KEROSENE	A thin oil used as fuel
KNOLL	Small, rounded hill
LINDBERGHS	Charles and Ann, whose baby was stolen
LONGING	Yearning or desire
MASH	Mixture from which alcohol can be distilled

MIGRANTS	Workers who travel around seeking work
MOLDY	Musty or stale in odor or taste
MOONSHINE	Illegally distilled whiskey
MOTTLED	Marked by spots or blotches
MUCK	Moist, sticky mixture, especially of mud and filth
PANDOWDY	Dish baked with sugar with thick top crust

PANHANDLE	Narrow strip of land projecting from a larger area
PARCHED	Extremely dry; exposed to heat
PRAIRIE	Large area of flat or rolling grassland
PROSPECTS	Chances; possibilities
QUINTUPLET	One of five offspring born in a single birth
REVENGE	Punishment in return for insult or injury

REVUE	A musical show
SASSY	Impudent; brashly bold
SCOWL	Frown
SEARING	Scorching or burning the surface of
SHALE	Rock made of layers of sediment
SIDING	Short section of railroad track

SKETCH	Hasty or undetailed drawing or painting
SNATCHED	Seized or grabbed
SOD	Grass-covered surface soil held together by roots
SOOTHE	Calm; quiet; ease or relieve
SQUINTED	Looked at with eyes partly closed
STUBBLE	Short, stiff stalks that remain after harvesting

STUPOR	A state of reduced sensibility; a daze
TART	Sour
TESTY	Irritable; touchy
THISTLE	Weedy plants with prickly leaves and purple flowers
THROB	Pulsate; beat rapidly or violently
TUFTS	Short cluster of strands, as of hair or grass

TUMBLEWEED	Broken off plant that rolls around in the wind
WARPED	Bent; twisted
WHEEZY	Making a hoarse whistling sound
WHIRLING	Rotating rapidly; spinning
WHIRRED	Produced an airy, vibrating sound
WHITTLED	Reduced gradually

WINCE	Shrink back or start involuntarily, as in pain or distress
WITHERED	Dried up; shriveled

Out Of The Dust Vocabulary

TESTY	SOD	GLOWERING	SNATCHED	MOLDY
ANTISEPTIC	WARPED	MOONSHINE	PARCHED	HARVEST
WITHERED	GRIME	FREE SPACE	THROB	DESPERATE
INTENTIONS	MOTTLED	DEFORMED	CCC	CHAFED
STUPOR	MIGRANTS	WHIRRED	SEARING	MASH

Out Of The Dust Vocabulary

DUSTBOWL	DIVINING	FLINCH	TART	SKETCH
WHITTLED	DROUGHT	WINCE	FESTERED	THISTLE
HUNCHED	WHIRLING	FREE SPACE	GOPHERS	PANHANDLE
SIDING	IGNITE	REVUE	TUFTS	BRITTLE
DUNES	REVENGE	BOXCAR	TUMBLEWEED	WHEEZY

Out Of The Dust Vocabulary

PROSPECTS	WITHERED	GRIME	HOARDING	GOPHERS
WHIRRED	WHEEZY	DUNES	CCC	CHAFED
FLINCH	SASSY	FREE SPACE	STUPOR	PARCHED
HARVEST	THROB	WHIRLING	DISTRACTED	BRITTLE
KNOLL	INTENTIONS	BAWLING	HUNCHED	SCOWL

Out Of The Dust Vocabulary

MIGRANTS	WINCE	SOOTHE	JEALOUS	PANDOWDY
SHALE	MASH	DESPERATE	ANTISEPTIC	TART
PRAIRIE	COMBINES	FREE SPACE	LONGING	MOTTLED
WARPED	FESTERED	SQUINTED	EXPOSING	SIDING
SNATCHED	DIVINING	PANHANDLE	LINDBERGHS	BETROTHAL

Out Of The Dust Vocabulary

HARVEST	INTENTIONS	PARCHED	ANTISEPTIC	REVENGE
KEROSENE	JEALOUS	DIVINING	STUPOR	CCC
SHALE	MIGRANTS	FREE SPACE	DISTRACTED	BETROTHAL
MOLDY	WINCE	SKETCH	PROSPECTS	SCOWL
SOD	IGNITE	THISTLE	MOONSHINE	THROB

Out Of The Dust Vocabulary

MOTTLED	BRITTLE	CHAFED	COURT	CROUCHED
TUFTS	TESTY	HUNCHED	DAZZLED	WARPED
COMBINES	GOPHERS	FREE SPACE	WHITTLED	HOARDING
WHIRRED	MUCK	WITHERED	PANHANDLE	TART
WHIRLING	SNATCHED	SASSY	STUBBLE	BOXCAR

Out Of The Dust Vocabulary

SQUINTED	BRITTLE	REVENGE	SASSY	SOD
DUSTBOWL	WINCE	THROB	MIGRANTS	WHITTLED
GLOWERING	WHEEZY	FREE SPACE	TART	MOONSHINE
DEFORMED	HOARDING	JEALOUS	DUNES	WHIRLING
GLAZING	THISTLE	KNOLL	FESTERED	KEROSENE

Out Of The Dust Vocabulary

PARCHED	DAZZLED	QUINTUPLET	SEARING	LONGING
EXPOSING	SNATCHED	INTENTIONS	FLINCH	SHALE
DESPERATE	SKETCH	FREE SPACE	WARPED	BAWLING
PROSPECTS	PANDOWDY	SCOWL	TUFTS	TESTY
STUPOR	PANHANDLE	PRAIRIE	DISTRACTED	TUMBLEWEED

Out Of The Dust Vocabulary

IGNITE	MOONSHINE	SHALE	LONGING	WHEEZY
REVENGE	PANHANDLE	DIVINING	DISTRACTED	SCOWL
SNATCHED	THISTLE	FREE SPACE	WHIRRED	TUFTS
HUNCHED	COURT	WITHERED	WINCE	ANTISEPTIC
DEFORMED	SKETCH	SEARING	HOARDING	KEROSENE

Out Of The Dust Vocabulary

STUBBLE	DUSTBOWL	WHITTLED	LINDBERGHS	GLOWERING
GLAZING	BAWLING	INTENTIONS	DESPERATE	FLINCH
SASSY	SIDING	FREE SPACE	CCC	STUPOR
KNOLL	PANDOWDY	TART	THROB	DAZZLED
JEALOUS	PRAIRIE	MOLDY	SOOTHE	SQUINTED

Out Of The Dust Vocabulary

ANTISEPTIC	LONGING	TUFTS	THROB	DAZZLED
DISTRACTED	SIDING	GRIME	SCOWL	HUNCHED
HOARDING	MUCK	FREE SPACE	BETROTHAL	SQUINTED
WITHERED	MIGRANTS	WHITTLED	GOPHERS	SEARING
SOOTHE	HARVEST	INTENTIONS	THISTLE	FESTERED

Out Of The Dust Vocabulary

JEALOUS	TART	STUBBLE	BOXCAR	TESTY
EXPOSING	DEFORMED	BRITTLE	MOTTLED	DUSTBOWL
DESPERATE	WHEEZY	FREE SPACE	GLAZING	STUPOR
SASSY	SHALE	DIVINING	SKETCH	LINDBERGHS
QUINTUPLET	FLINCH	WARPED	MASH	MOLDY

Out Of The Dust Vocabulary

TESTY	PARCHED	STUPOR	WHIRRED	DIVINING
SOOTHE	INTENTIONS	IGNITE	PANDOWDY	MUCK
DESPERATE	SASSY	FREE SPACE	MOLDY	SNATCHED
LONGING	JEALOUS	TUFTS	STUBBLE	BOXCAR
SEARING	DEFORMED	MOTTLED	PROSPECTS	FESTERED

Out Of The Dust Vocabulary

GLAZING	HARVEST	WHEEZY	CROUCHED	LINDBERGHS
GOPHERS	DISTRACTED	REVENGE	DAZZLED	DUNES
BAWLING	SCOWL	FREE SPACE	MIGRANTS	PRAIRIE
REVUE	WINCE	CHAFED	TART	WHIRLING
COURT	THISTLE	BETROTHAL	QUINTUPLET	KNOLL

Out Of The Dust Vocabulary

GRIME	FLINCH	CCC	TESTY	SOD
TUMBLEWEED	MOTTLED	DUNES	WHEEZY	STUBBLE
STUPOR	MIGRANTS	FREE SPACE	BAWLING	MOONSHINE
LONGING	FESTERED	WARPED	CROUCHED	DAZZLED
ANTISEPTIC	PROSPECTS	REVUE	WHITTLED	SNATCHED

Out Of The Dust Vocabulary

HOARDING	TUFTS	GLOWERING	BETROTHAL	DISTRACTED
SQUINTED	MOLDY	DIVINING	LINDBERGHS	COMBINES
REVENGE	MUCK	FREE SPACE	GLAZING	KEROSENE
DESPERATE	DUSTBOWL	CHAFED	BOXCAR	WINCE
SKETCH	PANDOWDY	EXPOSING	GOPHERS	SHALE

Out Of The Dust Vocabulary

CCC	LINDBERGHS	DEFORMED	MASH	JEALOUS
MOLDY	PRAIRIE	HUNCHED	INTENTIONS	CROUCHED
SEARING	SKETCH	FREE SPACE	MIGRANTS	MOONSHINE
TUMBLEWEED	WITHERED	REVENGE	COURT	BRITTLE
SNATCHED	STUBBLE	SOOTHE	GRIME	BOXCAR

Out Of The Dust Vocabulary

FLINCH	DESPERATE	KNOLL	TART	GLOWERING
HARVEST	HOARDING	SQUINTED	DAZZLED	THROB
GOPHERS	PARCHED	FREE SPACE	SCOWL	LONGING
SIDING	REVUE	DROUGHT	SASSY	WHIRLING
DUNES	SOD	WINCE	WHITTLED	KEROSENE

Out Of The Dust Vocabulary

WARPED	KEROSENE	DUNES	TESTY	WHIRRED
TART	PARCHED	WHITTLED	REVENGE	STUBBLE
DROUGHT	GLOWERING	FREE SPACE	BAWLING	DAZZLED
SEARING	SKETCH	THROB	BOXCAR	TUFTS
MOONSHINE	SIDING	SOOTHE	PANHANDLE	ANTISEPTIC

Out Of The Dust Vocabulary

GRIME	JEALOUS	THISTLE	QUINTUPLET	LINDBERGHS
LONGING	MUCK	WHEEZY	SASSY	SHALE
WITHERED	PRAIRIE	FREE SPACE	WHIRLING	BRITTLE
COMBINES	STUPOR	DUSTBOWL	PROSPECTS	GOPHERS
PANDOWDY	MIGRANTS	MOLDY	CCC	KNOLL

Out Of The Dust Vocabulary

THISTLE	SOD	BRITTLE	STUBBLE	STUPOR
DUSTBOWL	BAWLING	SEARING	FLINCH	PRAIRIE
COURT	PANHANDLE	FREE SPACE	LONGING	WHIRRED
WARPED	EXPOSING	TART	PARCHED	MOLDY
REVENGE	WITHERED	INTENTIONS	MUCK	HARVEST

Out Of The Dust Vocabulary

WHEEZY	SCOWL	QUINTUPLET	GLOWERING	MASH
REVUE	DIVINING	SIDING	GOPHERS	THROB
DESPERATE	WHIRLING	FREE SPACE	DUNES	MOONSHINE
COMBINES	DISTRACTED	DAZZLED	MIGRANTS	KEROSENE
IGNITE	KNOLL	SHALE	SKETCH	ANTISEPTIC

Out Of The Dust Vocabulary

PANDOWDY	SHALE	DUSTBOWL	FESTERED	CROUCHED
WHEEZY	COURT	HARVEST	PANHANDLE	BOXCAR
TUMBLEWEED	SCOWL	FREE SPACE	STUPOR	REVUE
PRAIRIE	DESPERATE	WARPED	FLINCH	DIVINING
MIGRANTS	TART	HUNCHED	CHAFED	WINCE

Out Of The Dust Vocabulary

JEALOUS	GOPHERS	KNOLL	BRITTLE	LONGING
SASSY	DROUGHT	ANTISEPTIC	MOONSHINE	SNATCHED
WHITTLED	WHIRLING	FREE SPACE	GLOWERING	EXPOSING
TESTY	MOTTLED	SEARING	DUNES	COMBINES
CCC	QUINTUPLET	SOD	MASH	SKETCH

Out Of The Dust Vocabulary

LONGING	DESPERATE	SOOTHE	GRIME	GOPHERS
JEALOUS	FESTERED	HARVEST	WARPED	REVUE
QUINTUPLET	BOXCAR	FREE SPACE	DUSTBOWL	CCC
SCOWL	STUBBLE	WHEEZY	SASSY	GLAZING
SHALE	WINCE	SNATCHED	LINDBERGHS	WHIRLING

Out Of The Dust Vocabulary

BRITTLE	STUPOR	CROUCHED	BAWLING	THROB
EXPOSING	TESTY	MASH	MUCK	GLOWERING
KNOLL	DUNES	FREE SPACE	TUFTS	DROUGHT
MOONSHINE	COURT	PARCHED	SQUINTED	PROSPECTS
HOARDING	THISTLE	TART	SEARING	DEFORMED

Out Of The Dust Vocabulary

WITHERED	EXPOSING	WHIRLING	BAWLING	REVENGE
SKETCH	WARPED	THROB	SOOTHE	SASSY
MUCK	DUNES	FREE SPACE	KEROSENE	TUFTS
BETROTHAL	KNOLL	SOD	SQUINTED	GRIME
WHITTLED	REVUE	COURT	MIGRANTS	SEARING

Out Of The Dust Vocabulary

DEFORMED	PRAIRIE	DAZZLED	WINCE	THISTLE
MOONSHINE	PANDOWDY	BOXCAR	SCOWL	FESTERED
TUMBLEWEED	GLOWERING	FREE SPACE	WHIRRED	HARVEST
DROUGHT	TESTY	SIDING	DUSTBOWL	SHALE
DISTRACTED	CHAFED	PARCHED	WHEEZY	COMBINES

Out Of The Dust Vocabulary

DEFORMED	MOLDY	SOD	DISTRACTED	LINDBERGHS
HUNCHED	SHALE	WITHERED	MOONSHINE	REVENGE
DESPERATE	WHIRRED	FREE SPACE	BOXCAR	KEROSENE
SNATCHED	WARPED	INTENTIONS	GOPHERS	DAZZLED
BAWLING	SASSY	WINCE	BETROTHAL	PARCHED

Out Of The Dust Vocabulary

CCC	PROSPECTS	SCOWL	WHEEZY	DROUGHT
JEALOUS	STUPOR	HOARDING	TART	GRIME
FLINCH	COURT	FREE SPACE	IGNITE	BRITTLE
EXPOSING	SQUINTED	MASH	SEARING	SIDING
GLOWERING	LONGING	THROB	PANHANDLE	TUMBLEWEED

Out Of The Dust Vocabulary

DEFORMED	REVUE	INTENTIONS	TUMBLEWEED	GOPHERS
DIVINING	BETROTHAL	TART	REVENGE	HUNCHED
PANDOWDY	GLOWERING	FREE SPACE	STUBBLE	QUINTUPLET
COURT	HOARDING	THROB	IGNITE	DAZZLED
SKETCH	CCC	WHITTLED	WHIRLING	ANTISEPTIC

Out Of The Dust Vocabulary

SASSY	SQUINTED	WARPED	MASH	PARCHED
BOXCAR	KEROSENE	DROUGHT	SNATCHED	SCOWL
SOOTHE	FLINCH	FREE SPACE	HARVEST	DISTRACTED
FESTERED	WINCE	SEARING	THISTLE	MOTTLED
PRAIRIE	SIDING	SHALE	LINDBERGHS	MOONSHINE